Washington Real Estate Test

Washington Estate License Exam: Best Test Prep Book to Help You Get Your License!

The Ultimate Workbook: Salesperson and Broker Exam-Passing Strategies

Table of Content

Introduction

Welcome to the World of Washington Real Estate

If you're reading this, chances are you're either considering or have already decided to embark on a career in real estate in the beautiful state of Washington. First and foremost, congratulations! You're about to enter a dynamic, rewarding field that offers endless opportunities for growth, both personally and professionally. Whether you're a complete novice or a seasoned professional looking to expand your expertise, this book is designed to be your comprehensive guide through every step of your journey.

Why Washington?

Washington State offers a unique blend of natural beauty and economic opportunity. From the bustling tech hub of Seattle to the serene landscapes of the Olympic Peninsula, Washington's real estate market is as diverse as its geography. The state's robust economy, driven by industries like technology, aerospace, and clean energy, has made it a hotspot for real estate activity. This book will delve into the specifics of the Washington real estate market, providing you with a nuanced understanding that will be invaluable as you begin your career.

What This Book Covers

This book is structured to provide a holistic view of real estate practice in Washington. We'll start by exploring the state's real estate market, discussing key economic indicators, property types, and market trends. From there, we'll move on to the nitty-gritty details of becoming a licensed real estate agent in Washington, including eligibility criteria, the application process, and what to expect on the exam day.

We'll also cover essential topics like property ownership, land use controls, laws of agency, property valuation, and financing. Specialized areas like commercial real estate, property management, and real estate investments will also be discussed in depth. And because ethics and legal considerations are crucial in any profession, we'll devote an entire chapter to these topics.

Who This Book is For

This book is for anyone who aspires to succeed in the Washington real estate industry. Whether you're a college student considering your career options, a professional looking for a career change, or an experienced real estate agent aiming to expand your knowledge, this book has something for you.

How to Use This Book

While you can read this book from start to finish, it's also designed to be a reference guide. Feel free to jump to specific chapters or sections that are most relevant to you. Each chapter ends with key takeaways and practice questions to help reinforce your understanding and prepare you for the Washington Real Estate License Exam.

Your Journey Begins Now

As you turn the page to the first chapter, you're taking a significant step toward a successful career in Washington real estate. We're thrilled to be part of your journey and are committed to providing you with the most comprehensive, up-to-date information possible. So, without further ado, let's dive in and start building the foundation for your future success in the Washington real estate market.

Understanding the Washington Real Estate Market

Understanding the real estate market in Washington is crucial for anyone aspiring to become a successful real estate agent in the state. The market is influenced by a myriad of factors, from economic indicators to geographical features, and understanding these elements can give you a significant edge. This chapter aims to provide a comprehensive overview of the Washington real estate market, focusing on key aspects that every aspiring and practicing real estate agent should know.

The Economic Landscape

Tech Industry Influence

Washington is home to some of the world's leading tech companies, including Microsoft and Amazon. The presence of these tech giants has a significant impact on the real estate market, especially in areas like Seattle and Bellevue. High-paying tech jobs attract a skilled workforce, which in turn drives up the demand for housing, both rental and owned.

Aerospace and Manufacturing

Boeing is another major player in Washington's economy, particularly affecting the real estate market around Everett. The aerospace industry's influence extends to the commercial real estate sector, with demand for industrial spaces and offices.

Tourism and Hospitality

Tourism is a significant contributor to Washington's economy, especially in cities like Spokane and tourist destinations like the San Juan Islands. This sector influences the market for vacation rentals and second homes.

Geographical Influences

Urban vs. Rural

Washington State offers a mix of urban and rural settings, each with its unique real estate characteristics. While urban areas like Seattle and Tacoma see high demand for apartments and condos, rural areas offer larger properties, including farmlands and waterfront homes.

Natural Beauty

The state's diverse geography, including mountains, forests, and coastlines, also plays a role in property valuation. Waterfront properties along the Puget Sound or homes with mountain views often command higher prices.

Market Trends

Housing Affordability

Despite the booming economy, housing affordability remains a concern, especially in cities like Seattle. The high demand and low supply have driven up prices, making it challenging for middle-income families to afford homes.

Gentrification

Areas like Capitol Hill in Seattle are undergoing gentrification, affecting property values and the demographic makeup of these neighborhoods. Understanding these trends can help agents identify investment opportunities for their clients.

Green Living

Washington is known for its eco-conscious population, and this is reflected in the real estate market. Properties with energy-efficient features or those close to public transit often attract a premium.

Property Types

Residential

The residential market is diverse, offering everything from high-rise condos to single-family homes. Suburban areas like Kirkland and Redmond are popular among families, while urban dwellers often prefer neighborhoods like Seattle's Capitol Hill.

Commercial

The commercial market is equally varied, with opportunities in retail, office space, and industrial properties. Understanding the zoning laws is crucial when dealing in commercial real estate.

Specialized Properties

Washington also offers specialized property types like vineyards in the Yakima Valley or vacation rentals in tourist hotspots like Leavenworth.

Legal and Regulatory Environment

Zoning Laws

Zoning laws in Washington can be complex, varying from one municipality to another. These laws affect property usage, and understanding them is crucial for any real estate transaction.

Rent Control and Tenant Laws

Washington has specific laws governing tenant rights and rent control. Being well-versed in these can help you serve your clients better, whether they are landlords or tenants.

Investment Opportunities

Fixer-Uppers

The market for fixer-uppers is vibrant in Washington, especially in older neighborhoods. These properties offer excellent opportunities for investors willing to put in the work to renovate and sell or rent.

Commercial Investments

With a booming economy, commercial properties offer lucrative investment opportunities. Areas around tech hubs are particularly promising for office space investments.

Conclusion

Understanding the Washington real estate market is a multi-faceted endeavor. From economic indicators to market trends and legal considerations, various factors influence the market. As a real estate agent, your ability to understand and navigate these complexities will be crucial in serving your clients effectively and succeeding in your career.

By grasping the nuances of the Washington real estate market, you'll be better equipped to offer valuable advice, spot investment opportunities, and ultimately, close successful deals. This chapter serves as a foundation, but remember, the real estate market is dynamic, and staying updated is key to long-term success.

Eligibility Criteria

Becoming a licensed real estate agent in Washington State is a multi-step process that begins with fulfilling specific eligibility criteria. This chapter aims to provide a comprehensive guide on the qualifications you need to meet, the educational requirements, and other essential prerequisites to set you on the path to a successful real estate career in Washington.

Age and Legal Status

Age Requirement

The first and most straightforward criterion is age. You must be at least 18 years old to apply for a real estate license in Washington State.

U.S. Citizenship or Legal Residency

While U.S. citizenship is not a requirement, you must be a legal resident. Non-citizens will need to provide proof of legal residency status, such as a Green Card or an appropriate visa.

Educational Requirements

Pre-License Education

Before applying for the exam, you must complete 90 hours of approved real estate education within two years before the exam date. This education is divided into a 60-hour course in Real Estate Fundamentals and a 30-hour course in Real Estate Practices.

Accredited Institutions

The courses must be taken from an accredited institution approved by the Washington State Department of Licensing (DOL). Many schools offer these courses both online and in-person.

Course Completion Certificates

Upon completing these courses, you will receive certificates of completion, which you will need to submit during the application process. Keep these certificates safe, as losing them can result in delays.

Background Check and Fingerprinting

Criminal History

Washington State requires a background check for all real estate license applicants. A criminal record does not automatically disqualify you, but certain offenses, such as fraud or violent crimes, may.

Fingerprinting

Fingerprinting is also a requirement and is usually done during the application process. The fingerprints are used to conduct a state and national background check.

Financial Responsibility

Credit Score

Washington State does not require a specific credit score, but a good credit history can make the business aspects of being a real estate agent, such as getting business loans, easier.

Financial Statements

Some brokerages may require financial statements to ensure you have the means to sustain yourself during the initial phase of your career, where income can be irregular.

Professional Competency

Broker Affiliation

Before your license is activated, you must be sponsored by an actively licensed Washington broker. This broker will guide you through the initial stages of your career and provide necessary on-the-job training.

Experience

While not a requirement for the license, some brokerages prefer agents with some experience in sales, marketing, or customer service. This experience can be beneficial when you start working.

Application Process

Online Application

Once you meet all the eligibility criteria, you can apply for the license online through the Washington State Department of Licensing website. The application will ask for details like your educational qualifications, background information, and broker affiliation.

Fees

There is an application fee that you must pay when submitting your application. This fee is non-refundable and varies depending on the type of license you are applying for.

Exam Eligibility

Exam Application

After your application is reviewed and accepted, you will be eligible to sit for the Washington real estate license exam. You will receive an exam eligibility notice, which you must present at the exam center.

Exam Fees

There is a separate fee for the exam, which you will need to pay when scheduling your test. This fee is also non-refundable.

Conclusion

Meeting the eligibility criteria is the first crucial step in your journey to becoming a licensed real estate agent in Washington State. From age and educational requirements to background checks and professional affiliations, each criterion serves to ensure that you are well-prepared for the responsibilities that come with the role. Failure to meet any of these requirements can result in delays or disqualification, so it's essential to understand and prepare for each one thoroughly.

By fulfilling these eligibility criteria diligently, you not only pave the way for a smooth application process but also lay a strong foundation for a successful and fulfilling career in real estate.

Application Process

The application process for obtaining a real estate license in Washington State is a multi-faceted journey that requires careful planning, attention to detail, and a thorough understanding of the state's specific requirements. This chapter aims to guide you through each step, from initial preparations to submitting your application, ensuring that you are well-equipped to navigate this crucial phase in your real estate career.

Preparing for the Application

Checklist of Requirements

Before diving into the application process, it's essential to prepare a checklist of all the requirements you need to fulfill. This list should include:

Proof of Age and Legal Residency

Educational Certificates

Background Check and Fingerprinting

Broker Affiliation Details

Application Fees

Organizing Documents

Having all your documents organized will make the application process smoother. Create separate folders for educational certificates, identification documents, and other necessary paperwork.

Budgeting for Fees

The application process involves various fees, including the application fee, exam fee, and fingerprinting costs. Budget for these to avoid any financial hiccups.

Online Registration and Account Setup

Creating an Account

The first step in the application process is to create an account on the Washington State Department of Licensing (DOL) website. This account will be your primary portal for all interactions with the DOL.

Personal Information

During account setup, you'll be required to provide personal information, including your full name, address, and Social Security number. Make sure all the information is accurate to avoid complications later.

Completing the Application Form

Accessing the Form

Once your account is set up, you can access the real estate license application form through the DOL's online portal.

Sections of the Form

The application form is divided into several sections, each requiring specific information:

Personal Details: Basic information such as name, date of birth, and contact details.
Educational Qualifications: Information about your pre-license education, including the names of the courses and the institutions where you completed them.
Legal Residency: Proof of legal residency or citizenship status.
Background Check: Details about your criminal history, if applicable.
Broker Affiliation: Information about your sponsoring broker.

Declaration: A series of legal declarations and consents.

Uploading Documents

You'll need to upload scanned copies of all required documents, such as educational certificates and proof of legal residency. Ensure that all scans are clear and legible.

Background Check and Fingerprinting

Scheduling an Appointment

After submitting the application form, you'll need to schedule an appointment for fingerprinting, which is essential for the background check.

The Fingerprinting Process

At the appointment, your fingerprints will be taken and submitted for a state and federal background check. This process usually takes a few weeks.

Payment of Fees

Application Fee

The application fee is mandatory and non-refundable. It can be paid online through the DOL portal.

Additional Fees

Apart from the application fee, you may also need to pay for fingerprinting and the background check. These fees vary and should be checked in advance.

Review and Submission

Double-Checking Information

Before submitting your application, double-check all the information and documents to ensure they are accurate and complete.

Final Submission

Once you're confident that everything is in order, you can proceed to submit your application. You'll receive a confirmation email upon successful submission.

Post-Submission Steps

Tracking Your Application

You can track the status of your application through the DOL portal. It's crucial to monitor this regularly and respond promptly to any queries or additional requirements from the DOL.

Receiving Exam Eligibility

Upon successful review of your application, you'll receive an exam eligibility notice, allowing you to schedule your licensing exam.

Conclusion

The application process for a real estate license in Washington State is a comprehensive and detailed procedure that requires meticulous preparation and execution. From setting up your online account to submitting your application and tracking its status, each step is crucial for advancing in your real estate career. By understanding the intricacies of this process and preparing accordingly, you can ensure a smoother, more efficient path to obtaining your Washington real estate license.

Exam Format

The Washington State Real Estate License Exam is a critical milestone on your path to becoming a licensed real estate professional. This chapter will provide an in-depth look at the exam format, including the types of questions you'll encounter, the subjects covered, and the strategies you can employ to maximize your chances of success.

Overview of the Exam

Structure

The Washington State Real Estate License Exam is divided into two main sections:

1. National Portion: This section tests your understanding of general real estate principles and practices that apply across the United States.
2. State Portion: This section focuses on real estate laws, regulations, and practices specific to Washington State.

Duration and Number of Questions

National Portion: 80 questions, 120 minutes
State Portion: 30 questions, 60 minutes

Scoring and Passing Criteria

National Portion: 75% or higher to pass
State Portion: 70% or higher to pass

Types of Questions

Multiple-Choice Questions

The exam consists entirely of multiple-choice questions, each with four answer options. You must choose the most accurate answer.

Scenario-Based Questions

Some questions will present you with a scenario and ask you to make a decision based on the information provided.

True or False

Though rare, you may encounter questions that require a simple true or false answer.

Subjects Covered

National Portion

Property Ownership and Land Use Controls: Understanding different types of ownership and land use policies.

Laws of Agency: The legal relationships between agents and principals.

Valuation and Market Analysis: How properties are valued and how market analysis is conducted.

Financing: Different types of loans and financing options available for real estate transactions.

State Portion

Washington State Laws and Regulations: Specific laws governing real estate in Washington.

Contract Laws: Understanding the state-specific contract laws that apply to real estate transactions.

State Tax Laws: Property taxes, transfer taxes, and other state-specific tax considerations.

Exam Day Procedures

What to Bring

Government-issued photo ID

Exam confirmation letter or email

Two #2 pencils

What Not to Bring

Electronic devices

Notes or study materials

Food or drinks

During the Exam

You will be monitored via video and audio.

Bathroom breaks are allowed but discouraged as the clock will not stop.

Strategies for Success

Time Management

Allocate specific time blocks for each section.

Don't spend too much time on a single question.

Elimination Technique

Eliminate obviously incorrect answers to improve your odds of selecting the correct one.

Flagging Questions

If unsure about a question, flag it and return to it later if time permits.

Review

Use any remaining time to review your answers, focusing first on questions you've flagged.

Post-Exam Procedures

Receiving Your Score

You will receive a preliminary score immediately after completing the exam. Official scores will be mailed to you within 5-7 business days.

Retaking the Exam

If you fail, you can retake the exam, but you must wait for a specific period and may need to pay a re-examination fee.

Conclusion

Understanding the format of the Washington State Real Estate License Exam is crucial for effective preparation and successful performance. This chapter has provided a comprehensive overview of what to expect, from the types of questions and subjects covered to exam day procedures and strategies for success. With diligent preparation and a clear understanding of the exam format, you are well on your way to becoming a licensed real estate professional in Washington State.

Property Ownership and Land Use Controls

Understanding the nuances of property ownership and land use controls is a cornerstone of real estate practice, especially in Washington State. This chapter aims to provide an in-depth understanding of the various types of property ownership, land use regulations, and zoning laws that are particularly relevant in this state. Whether you're an aspiring real estate agent, a seasoned investor, or someone looking to buy their first home, this chapter will equip you with the knowledge you need to navigate the complex landscape of property ownership and land use controls.

Types of Property Ownership

Fee Simple Absolute

In a Fee Simple Absolute ownership, the owner has the most extensive set of rights and privileges over the property. They can sell, lease, or pass the property to heirs without any conditions. In Washington, this is the most common form of property ownership and is often the most sought after because of the freedom it offers.

Implications in Washington

Washington State law allows for the unencumbered transfer of fee simple property, but it's essential to understand that even fee simple properties are subject to taxation, eminent domain, and police power regulations.

Life Estate

A life estate is an interest in real property that is limited to the duration of someone's life, often the person holding the life estate. Upon their death, the property reverts to a predetermined individual, known as the "remainderman."

Implications in Washington

In Washington, life estates are often used in estate planning to avoid probate. The life tenant has the responsibility to maintain the property but cannot make significant changes without the consent of the remainderman.

Leasehold Estate

A leasehold estate is a temporary ownership where the tenant has the right to occupy and use the property for a specified period, usually in exchange for rent.

Implications in Washington

Washington State has specific laws governing the rights and responsibilities of both landlords and tenants, including regulations on rent control, eviction procedures, and maintenance.

Joint Tenancy and Tenancy in Common

Joint tenancy involves two or more individuals owning a property with equal shares. In contrast, tenants in common can own unequal shares of a property.

Implications in Washington

Washington State allows for both joint tenancy and tenancy in common, but it's crucial to specify the type of ownership in the property deed to avoid legal complications.

Community Property

Washington is one of the few community property states, meaning that property acquired during a marriage is considered owned by both spouses equally.

Implications in Washington

In the event of a divorce, community property laws can significantly impact asset division. It's crucial to consult a legal advisor familiar with Washington's community property laws when dealing with marital assets.

Land Use Controls

Zoning Laws

Zoning laws are regulations that dictate how property in specific geographic zones can be used.

Washington State Zoning

In Washington, local governments have the authority to enact zoning laws. For example, Seattle has multiple zoning categories, including Single-Family Residential, Multi-Family Residential, Commercial, Industrial, and Mixed-Use.

Building Codes

Building codes are sets of rules that specify the minimum acceptable levels of safety for constructed objects.

Washington State Building Codes

Washington State has adopted the International Building Code (IBC), but local municipalities may have additional regulations. It's crucial to consult local codes when planning construction.

Environmental Restrictions

Washington State has stringent environmental laws affecting land use, especially in areas near water bodies or protected lands.

Critical Areas Ordinance in Washington

Washington's Critical Areas Ordinance protects wetlands, fish and wildlife habitat conservation areas, and frequently flooded areas. Property owners must adhere to these regulations, which may include maintaining buffer zones around critical areas.

Historic Preservation

Some areas in Washington, like parts of Spokane and Tacoma, have historic districts where property owners face additional restrictions.

Washington State Historic Preservation Office

The Washington State Historic Preservation Office (SHPO) is responsible for maintaining the Washington Heritage Register, a list of historically significant properties.

Case Studies

Case Study 1: Seattle's Upzoning

Seattle recently underwent an "upzoning" process to allow for more high-density housing. This has implications for property values and opportunities for development.

Case Study 2: Spokane's Historic Districts

Spokane has several historic districts where property owners face additional restrictions. Understanding these can be crucial for potential investors or developers.

Conclusion

Understanding property ownership and land use controls is crucial for anyone involved in the real estate industry in Washington State. This chapter has provided a comprehensive overview, from the types of property ownership to the various land use controls like zoning laws and environmental restrictions. Armed with this knowledge, you're better prepared to navigate the complexities of the Washington real estate market.

Mock Exam Property Ownership and Land Use Controls

➡1. What is the most complete form of ownership?

   A. Life Estate

   B. Leasehold Estate

   C. Fee Simple Absolute

   D. Joint Tenancy

   Answer: C. Fee Simple Absolute

   Fee Simple Absolute grants the owner all rights to the property, including the ability to sell, lease, or will it to heirs.

➡2. What does a life estate provide?

   A. Complete control of the property

   B. Ownership for the duration of someone's life

   C. Equal ownership among spouses

   D. Ownership for a specified period

   Answer: B. Ownership for the duration of someone's life

   A life estate grants ownership for the duration of someone's life, usually the life tenant. Upon their death, the property reverts to the original owner or a designated remainderman.

➡3. What is the primary advantage of a Leasehold Estate?

   A. Equity build-up

   B. Lower upfront costs

   C. Complete control

   D. Right of survivorship

Answer: B. Lower upfront costs

The primary advantage of a Leasehold Estate is lower upfront costs. The tenant has the right to occupy and use the property for a specified period, but ownership remains with the landlord.

→4. What is unique about Joint Tenancy?

A. Unequal shares

B. No right of survivorship

C. Equal shares and right of survivorship

D. Complete control of the property

Answer: C. Equal shares and right of survivorship

Joint tenancy involves two or more people owning property with equal shares and the right of survivorship.

→5. In which states is Community Property a common form of ownership?

A. All states

B. Only in community property states

C. Only in common law states

D. None of the above

Answer: B. Only in community property states

Community Property is a form of ownership common in community property states, where any property acquired during a marriage is considered jointly owned by both spouses.

→6. What is the primary purpose of zoning laws?

A. To control property taxes

B. To regulate land use

C. To establish school districts

D. To determine property value

Answer: B. To regulate land use

Zoning laws are enacted by local governments to regulate how land can be used in specific areas.

➡7. **What is eminent domain?**

A. The right to lease property

B. The right of the government to take private property for public use

C. The right to inherit property

D. The right to sell property

Answer: B. The right of the government to take private property for public use

Eminent domain is the power of the government to take private property for public use, usually with compensation to the owner.

➡8. **What is a variance in the context of land use?**

A. A change in property value

B. A change in zoning laws

C. Permission to use land in a way that is prohibited by zoning laws

D. A change in property taxes

Answer: C. Permission to use land in a way that is prohibited by zoning laws

A variance is special permission granted by a zoning authority to use land in a manner that is generally not allowed under current zoning laws.

➡9. **What is a restrictive covenant?**

A. A government-imposed restriction on land use

B. A privately imposed agreement that restricts the use of land

C. A restriction on the sale of property

D. A restriction on leasing property

Answer: B. A privately imposed agreement that restricts the use of land

A restrictive covenant is an agreement that limits how a property owner can use their property, usually to preserve the value and integrity of a neighborhood.

➡**10. What is the difference between real property and personal property?**

A. Real property can be moved, but personal property cannot

B. Real property is land and anything permanently attached to it, while personal property is movable

C. Real property is always more valuable

D. There is no difference

Answer: B. Real property is land and anything permanently attached to it, while personal property is movable

Real property refers to land and anything permanently attached to it, like buildings. Personal property refers to movable items like furniture and cars.

➡**11. What is a buffer zone in land use planning?**

A. An area between residential and commercial zones

B. An area reserved for parks

C. An area where any type of construction is allowed

D. An area reserved for schools

Answer: A. An area between residential and commercial zones

A buffer zone is an area that separates different types of land uses, like residential and commercial, to reduce conflict between them.

➠12. **What is the main goal of sustainable development?**

A. To maximize profits

B. To use resources in a way that meets current needs without compromising future needs

C. To develop as quickly as possible

D. To use all available land

Answer: B. To use resources in a way that meets current needs without compromising future needs

Sustainable development aims to meet the needs of the present without compromising the ability of future generations to meet their own needs.

➠13. **What is a master plan in the context of city planning?**

A. A detailed budget

B. A long-term planning document that guides future growth and development

C. A short-term plan for immediate construction

D. A plan for a single building

Answer: B. A long-term planning document that guides future growth and development

A master plan is a comprehensive long-term plan that outlines the vision, policies, and goals for future growth and development in a city or community.

➠14. **What is the main purpose of a building permit?**

A. To raise revenue for the city

B. To ensure that construction complies with local codes and ordinances

C. To limit the number of buildings in an area

D. To increase property values

Answer: B. To ensure that construction complies with local codes and ordinances

A building permit is required to ensure that any new construction or significant changes to existing structures comply with local building codes and regulations.

→15. What is the role of a property appraiser in land use?

A. To determine the highest and best use of a property

B. To enforce zoning laws

C. To issue building permits

D. To draft master plans

Answer: A. To determine the highest and best use of a property

A property appraiser assesses the value of a property based on its highest and best use, considering factors like location, zoning, and market conditions.

→16. What is the "Right to Farm" law?

A. A law that allows anyone to farm anywhere

B. A law that protects farmers from nuisance lawsuits

C. A law that restricts farming to certain zones

D. A law that bans farming in urban areas

Answer: B. A law that protects farmers from nuisance lawsuits

The "Right to Farm" law is designed to protect existing farmers from nuisance lawsuits filed by new neighbors who may not be accustomed to the operations of a farm.

→17. What does the term "infill development" refer to?

A. Developing farmland into residential areas

B. Developing open spaces in urban areas

C. Developing new structures on vacant or underused land within existing city boundaries

D. Expanding urban areas into rural zones

Answer: C. Developing new structures on vacant or underused land within existing city boundaries

Infill development aims to make use of vacant or underutilized lands within a built-up area for further construction or development.

➡18. What is a nonconforming use?

A. A use that conforms to current zoning laws but not to building codes

B. A use that was lawful before a zoning ordinance was passed but is no longer permitted

C. A use that violates both zoning laws and building codes

D. A use that is temporarily permitted due to a variance

Answer: B. A use that was lawful before a zoning ordinance was passed but is no longer permitted

A nonconforming use is a land use that was legal when established but does not conform to new or changed zoning laws.

➡19. What is the main purpose of a land trust?

A. To hold land for development

B. To preserve land for future generations

C. To generate revenue through land sales

D. To control land prices

Answer: B. To preserve land for future generations

A land trust is an organization that actively works to conserve land by undertaking or assisting in land or conservation easement acquisition.

➡20. What is "mixed-use development"?

A. Development that includes both residential and commercial properties

B. Development that is used for industrial purposes

C. Development that is only used for residential purposes

D. Development that is only used for commercial purposes

Answer: A. Development that includes both residential and commercial properties

Mixed-use development is a type of urban development that blends residential, commercial, cultural, institutional, or entertainment uses.

➡️**21. What is the primary purpose of a greenbelt?**

A. To provide recreational spaces

B. To separate urban areas from rural areas

C. To increase property values

D. To reduce air pollution

Answer: B. To separate urban areas from rural areas

A greenbelt is an area of largely undeveloped, wild, or agricultural land surrounding or neighboring urban areas.

➡️**22. What is "brownfield land"?**

A. Land that is used for agricultural purposes

B. Land that has been contaminated by hazardous waste

C. Land that is reserved for parks and recreation

D. Land that is zoned for industrial use

Answer: B. Land that has been contaminated by hazardous waste

Brownfield land is a term used in urban planning to describe any previously developed land that is not currently in use and may be potentially contaminated.

➡️**23. What does "highest and best use" mean in the context of real estate?**

A. The use that generates the most income

B. The use that is most suitable from a social perspective

C. The use that maximizes a property's value

D. The use that is most environmentally sustainable

Answer: C. The use that maximizes a property's value

"Highest and best use" is a real estate appraisal term for the most profitable, likely use of a property, which is physically possible, appropriately supported, and legally permissible.

➡24. What is "air rights"?

A. The right to unlimited views from a property

B. The right to the air above the land

C. The right to pollute the air

D. The right to fresh air

Answer: B. The right to the air above the land

Air rights are a type of development right in real estate, referring to the empty space above a property.

➡25. What is "land banking"?

A. The process of buying land as an investment

B. The process of rezoning land

C. The process of converting agricultural land to residential land

D. The process of accumulating land for future development

Answer: D. The process of accumulating land for future development

Land banking is the practice of aggregating parcels of land for future sale or development.

➡26. What is "eminent domain"?

A. The right of the government to tax property

B. The right of the government to seize private property for public use

C. The right of the property owner to change the zoning laws

D. The right of the property owner to deny access to government officials

Answer: B. The right of the government to seize private property for public use
Eminent domain is the power of the government to take private property and convert it into public use, often with compensation to the owner.

➡ **27. What is "spot zoning"?**

A. Zoning that changes frequently

B. Zoning that applies to a specific area within a larger zoned area

C. Zoning that applies only to commercial properties

D. Zoning that applies only during certain times of the year

Answer: B. Zoning that applies to a specific area within a larger zoned area
Spot zoning is the application of zoning laws that are different from the surrounding area, usually benefiting a single property owner.

➡ **28. What does "buffer zone" mean in the context of land use?**

A. An area that separates different types of land uses

B. An area that is restricted for military use

C. An area that is designated for future development

D. An area that is kept empty for aesthetic purposes

Answer: A. An area that separates different types of land uses
A buffer zone is a zonal area that lies between two or more other areas that are contrasting in nature.

➡ **29. What is "downzoning"?**

A. Changing the zoning of a property to a less intensive use

B. Changing the zoning of a property to a more intensive use

C. Rezoning to allow for higher buildings

D. Rezoning to allow for commercial use

Answer: A. Changing the zoning of a property to a less intensive use

Downzoning is the rezoning of land to a more restrictive zone to prevent overdevelopment.

➡ **30. What is "land grading"?**

A. The process of making land more level

B. The process of evaluating the quality of soil

C. The process of determining the value of the land

D. The process of rezoning land

Answer: A. The process of making land more level

Land grading is the act of leveling the surface of the soil to prepare it for construction or agriculture.

➡ **31. What is "land reclamation"?**

A. The process of converting developed land back to its natural state

B. The process of converting barren land into arable land

C. The process of restoring contaminated land

D. All of the above

Answer: D. All of the above

Land reclamation can involve converting barren land into arable land, restoring contaminated land, or converting developed land back to its natural state.

➡ **32. What is "land tenure"?**

A. The legal regime in which land is owned

B. The length of time land has been owned by a single entity

C. The tax status of a piece of land

D. The zoning classification of a piece of land

Answer: A. The legal regime in which land is owned

Land tenure is the way land is held or owned at the individual or collective level.

➡ **33. What is "land partition"?**

A. The division of a larger piece of land into smaller lots

B. The legal process to settle land disputes

C. The change of land zoning types

D. The process of land reclamation

Answer: A. The division of a larger piece of land into smaller lots

Land partition is the division of real property into two or more parcels.

➡ **34. What is "land speculation"?**

A. Buying land with the hope that its value will increase

B. Buying land for immediate development

C. Buying land for long-term investment

D. Buying land for agricultural use

Answer: A. Buying land with the hope that its value will increase

Land speculation is the purchase of land with the hope that it will increase in value for resale at a profit.

➡ **35. What is "land surveying"?**

A. The process of measuring land and its features

B. The process of evaluating the quality of soil

C. The process of determining the value of the land

D. The process of rezoning land

Answer: A. The process of measuring land and its features

Land surveying is the technique of determining the terrestrial or three-dimensional position of points and the distances and angles between them.

➡️**36. What is "inclusionary zoning"?**

A. Zoning that includes only residential properties

B. Zoning that mandates a portion of new development be affordable for low-income households

C. Zoning that includes only commercial properties

D. Zoning that includes only industrial properties

Answer: B. Zoning that mandates a portion of new development be affordable for low-income households

Inclusionary zoning is a regulation that requires a given share of new construction to be affordable for people with low to moderate incomes.

➡️**37. What is "land banking"?**

A. The process of buying land for immediate development

B. The process of holding onto land as a long-term investment

C. The process of using land as collateral for a loan

D. The process of converting barren land into arable land

Answer: B. The process of holding onto land as a long-term investment

Land banking is the practice of aggregating parcels of land for future sale or development.

➡️**38. What does "air rights" refer to?**

A. The right to unlimited height in building above a property

B. The right to clean air in a residential area

C. The right to the airspace above the physical property

D. The right to fly drones over a property

Answer: C. The right to the airspace above the physical property

Air rights are the property interest in the "space" above the earth's surface.

→39. What is "land assembly"?

A. The process of gathering various small parcels of land into a single larger parcel

B. The process of constructing a building on a piece of land

C. The process of converting barren land into arable land

D. The process of dividing a larger piece of land into smaller lots

Answer: A. The process of gathering various small parcels of land into a single larger parcel

Land assembly is the process by which smaller parcels of land are combined to create a single larger parcel.

→40. What is "land degradation"?

A. The process of land losing its productivity due to human activities

B. The process of land increasing in value

C. The process of land being rezoned for less intensive use

D. The process of land being converted into a natural reserve

Answer: A. The process of land losing its productivity due to human activities

Land degradation refers to the deterioration or loss of the productive capacity of the soils for present and future.

→41. What is "land improvement"?

A. The process of adding value to a land through developments like roads and utilities

B. The process of converting barren land into arable land

C. The process of rezoning land for more intensive use

D. The process of restoring contaminated land

Answer: A. The process of adding value to a land through developments like roads and utilities

Land improvement refers to the effort made to make land more usable and valuable.

➡42. **What is "land lease"?**

A. A contract where the landowner gives another the right to use land in exchange for rent

B. A contract to sell land

C. A contract to buy land

D. A contract to develop land

Answer: A. A contract where the landowner gives another the right to use land in exchange for rent

A land lease is an agreement where the landowner permits a tenant to use the land in exchange for rent.

➡43. **What is "land reservation"?**

A. Land set aside for future use

B. Land set aside for indigenous people

C. Land set aside for environmental protection

D. All of the above

Answer: D. All of the above

Land reservation can refer to land set aside for various purposes, including future use, protection of indigenous rights, or environmental conservation.

44. What is "land trust"?

A. A legal entity that holds the ownership of a land for the benefit of another party

B. A company that invests in land

C. A non-profit organization that protects land for future generations

D. A government agency that manages public lands

Answer: A. A legal entity that holds the ownership of a land for the benefit of another party

A land trust is a legal entity that takes ownership of, or authority over, a property at the behest of the property owner.

45. What is "land use planning"?

A. The process of managing land resources to prevent land degradation

B. The process of determining the best way to use land resources

C. The process of rezoning land

D. The process of converting barren land into arable land

Answer: B. The process of determining the best way to use land resources

Land use planning involves the systematic assessment of land and water potential, alternatives for land use, and the economic and social conditions.

46. What does "eminent domain" refer to?

A. The right of the government to take private property for public use

B. The right of a landlord to evict a tenant for non-payment of rent

C. The right of a property owner to develop their land as they see fit

D. The right of a tenant to enjoy their rented property without interference from the landlord

Answer: A. The right of the government to take private property for public use

Eminent domain is the power of the government to take private property and convert it into public use, usually with compensation to the owner.

➡️47. What is "adverse possession"?

  A. The illegal occupation of property

  B. The acquisition of property through inheritance

  C. The acquisition of property through a long-term, open, and notorious occupation

  D. The acquisition of property through a legal purchase

  Answer: C. The acquisition of property through a long-term, open, and notorious occupation

  Adverse possession is a legal principle that allows a person who possesses someone else's land for an extended period of time to claim legal title to that land.

➡️48. What is "land value tax"?

  A. A tax on the value of a building

  B. A tax on the value of land, excluding the value of buildings and improvements

  C. A tax on the sale of land

  D. A tax on the rental income from land

  Answer: B. A tax on the value of land, excluding the value of buildings and improvements

  A land value tax is a levy on the unimproved value of land.

➡️49. What is "landlocked property"?

  A. Property that is surrounded by other properties, with no direct access to a public road

  B. Property that is located far from any body of water

  C. Property that is not subject to flooding

  D. Property that is restricted from development

  Answer: A. Property that is surrounded by other properties, with no direct access to a public road

Landlocked property is real estate that has no direct access to a public street, so you can't get to it unless you go through someone else's property first.

➡ **50. What is "latent defect"?**

A. A defect that is obvious and easy to spot

B. A defect that is hidden and not immediately obvious

C. A defect that has been disclosed by the seller

D. A defect that has been repaired before the sale of the property

Answer: B. A defect that is hidden and not immediately obvious

A latent defect is a fault in the property that could not have been discovered by a reasonably thorough inspection before the sale.

Laws of Agency and Fiduciary Duties

Navigating the complex world of real estate transactions requires a deep understanding of the roles and responsibilities that come with being an agent. In Washington State, these roles are governed by specific laws and regulations aimed at ensuring that both buyers and sellers are represented fairly and ethically. This chapter will delve into the intricacies of agency laws and fiduciary duties, providing you with the knowledge you need to practice real estate in Washington State effectively and ethically.

The Essence of Agency in Real Estate

In real estate, an agency relationship is a legal bond between the agent and the client, be it a buyer or a seller. This relationship is founded on trust, and it obligates the agent to act in the best interests of the client. In Washington State, the law outlines several types of agency relationships, each with its own set of rules and responsibilities.

Seller's Agent

When you act as a seller's agent, your primary responsibility is to represent the seller's interests in the transaction. This involves a range of tasks, from listing and marketing the property to negotiating favorable terms for the seller. The fiduciary duties owed to the seller include loyalty, confidentiality, and full disclosure, among others.

Buyer's Agent

As a buyer's agent, your role is to represent the buyer in the real estate transaction. This involves understanding the buyer's needs, showing them suitable properties, and negotiating the best possible deal on their behalf. Like the seller's agent, you owe fiduciary duties to the buyer, which must be upheld throughout the transaction.

Dual Agency

Dual agency is a unique situation where you represent both the buyer and the seller in the same transaction. Washington State law allows for dual agency but requires explicit, written consent from both parties. In such cases, the agent must exercise extreme caution to maintain impartiality and uphold their fiduciary duties to both clients.

Fiduciary Duties: The Heart of Agency

Fiduciary duties are the set of responsibilities that an agent owes to their client. In Washington State, these duties are codified in law and serve as the foundation of the agency relationship.

Duty of Loyalty

The duty of loyalty requires you to act solely in your client's best interest, putting their needs above your own and those of any other parties involved in the transaction. This is the cornerstone of the fiduciary duties and serves as the guiding principle for all your actions as an agent.

Duty of Confidentiality

As an agent, you will be privy to a lot of confidential information about your client. The duty of confidentiality obligates you to safeguard this information and not disclose it to any third parties unless required by law or explicitly authorized by the client.

Duty of Full Disclosure

While you are required to maintain confidentiality, you also have a duty to disclose all material facts that could affect the transaction. This includes any information that could influence the client's decision to buy or sell, such as market conditions, the condition of the property, or the financial standing of the other party in the transaction.

Duty of Care

The duty of care requires you to exercise a high standard of care in all your dealings on behalf of the client. This means conducting thorough research, providing accurate information, and carrying out all tasks with the skill and expertise expected of a competent real estate agent.

Conclusion

Understanding and upholding your agency relationships and fiduciary duties is crucial for practicing real estate in Washington State. Failure to do so can result in legal repercussions and damage to your reputation. Therefore, it's essential to familiarize yourself with the laws and regulations governing these aspects of real estate practice, both for the sake of your clients and your career.

Mock Exam Laws of Agency and Fiduciary Duties

➡1. What is the primary role of an agent in a real estate transaction?

A. To represent the buyer only

B. To act on behalf of the principal

C. To market the property

D. To negotiate the best price for themselves

Answer: B

The primary role of an agent is to act on behalf of the principal, whether that's the buyer or the seller.

➡2. Which of the following is NOT a fiduciary duty an agent owes to their client?

A. Loyalty

B. Disclosure

C. Profit maximization

D. Confidentiality

Answer: C

Profit maximization is not a fiduciary duty. The fiduciary duties include loyalty, disclosure, and confidentiality among others.

➡3. What is dual agency?

A. When two agents represent a buyer

B. When an agent represents both buyer and seller

C. When two agents represent a seller

D. When an agent represents two buyers

Answer: B

Dual agency occurs when an agent represents both the buyer and the seller in a single transaction.

➡4. Which state law is most likely to govern real estate agency relationships?

A. Federal law

B. Common law

C. State-specific law

D. International law

Answer: C

Each state has its own set of laws and regulations governing real estate agency relationships.

➡5. What must an agent do if they are involved in a dual agency situation?

A. Keep it a secret

B. Get written consent from both parties

C. Represent the buyer's interests only

D. Represent the seller's interests only

Answer: B

In a dual agency situation, both parties must be made fully aware of the dual agency and consent to it in writing.

➡6. What does the fiduciary duty of "reasonable care and skill" entail?

A. Making the most money for the client

B. Acting as any competent agent would

C. Keeping all information confidential

D. Always being available for the client

Answer: B

The duty of "reasonable care and skill" means the agent must act as any competent agent would in the same situation.

➡7. What is the primary focus of the fiduciary duty of "loyalty"?

A. Maximizing profit for the agent

B. Putting the client's needs above the agent's

C. Keeping all information confidential

D. Disclosing all facts to the client

Answer: B

The fiduciary duty of "loyalty" requires the agent to always act in the best interest of their client.

➡8. What is the consequence of breaching fiduciary duties?

A. Loss of job

B. Legal liabilities

C. A warning

D. No consequences

Answer: B

Breaching fiduciary duties can result in various legal liabilities, including fines and loss of license.

➡9. What is the purpose of an agency agreement?

A. To outline the agent's commission

B. To outline the scope of the agent's responsibilities

C. To protect the agent from legal action

D. To list the properties for sale

Answer: B

An agency agreement outlines the scope of the agent's responsibilities and how they will be compensated.

➡10. Which of the following is NOT a type of agency relationship in real estate?

A. Seller's agent

B. Buyer's agent

C. Independent agent

D. Dual agent

Answer: C

"Independent agent" is not a standard type of agency relationship in real estate. The common types are seller's agent, buyer's agent, and dual agent.

➡11. What is the term for the person represented by an agent?

A. Client

B. Customer

C. Broker

D. Associate

Answer: A

The person represented by an agent is referred to as the client.

➡12. What is the fiduciary duty of "disclosure" primarily concerned with?

A. Revealing all known facts that materially affect the property

B. Keeping the client's information confidential

C. Making the most money for the client

D. Always being available for the client

Answer: A

The fiduciary duty of "disclosure" requires the agent to reveal all known facts that materially affect the property's value.

⟹ **13. What is the opposite of a dual agency?**

A. Single agency

B. Triple agency

C. No agency

D. Sub-agency

Answer: A

The opposite of a dual agency is a single agency, where the agent represents only one party in the transaction.

⟹ **14. What is the primary purpose of a buyer's agent?**

A. To represent the seller

B. To represent the buyer

C. To market the property

D. To negotiate the best price for themselves

Answer: B

The primary purpose of a buyer's agent is to represent the buyer's interests in the transaction.

⟹ **15. What is the fiduciary duty of "obedience" concerned with?**

A. Following all of the client's lawful instructions

B. Disclosing all material facts

C. Keeping all information confidential

D. Making the most money for the client

Answer: A

The fiduciary duty of "obedience" requires the agent to follow all lawful instructions from their client.

➡16. What is the primary role of a sub-agent?

A. To represent the buyer

B. To represent the seller

C. To assist the primary agent

D. To market the property

Answer: C

The primary role of a sub-agent is to assist the primary agent in fulfilling their duties.

➡17. What is the fiduciary duty of "accounting"?

A. Keeping track of all financial transactions

B. Disclosing all material facts

C. Keeping all information confidential

D. Making the most money for the client

Answer: A

The fiduciary duty of "accounting" requires the agent to keep track of all financial transactions related to the agency relationship.

➡18. What is the primary purpose of a listing agreement?

A. To outline the buyer's needs

B. To outline the scope of the agent's responsibilities towards the seller

C. To protect the agent from legal action

D. To list the properties for rent

Answer: B

A listing agreement outlines the scope of the agent's responsibilities towards the seller and how they will be compensated.

➟**19. What is the term for an agent who represents the seller?**

A. Buyer's agent

B. Seller's agent

C. Dual agent

D. Sub-agent

Answer: B

An agent who represents the seller is known as a seller's agent.

➟**20. What is the consequence of not disclosing a dual agency?**

A. Loss of job

B. Legal liabilities

C. A warning

D. No consequences

Answer: B

Failure to disclose a dual agency can result in legal liabilities, including fines and loss of license.

➟**21. What is the primary role of a transaction broker?**

A. To represent the buyer

B. To represent the seller

C. To facilitate the transaction without representing either party

D. To market the property

Answer: C

A transaction broker's primary role is to facilitate the real estate transaction without representing either the buyer or the seller.

➡22. What does the fiduciary duty of "loyalty" require?

A. Disclosing all material facts

B. Putting the client's interests above all others

C. Keeping all information confidential

D. Following all of the client's instructions

Answer: B

The fiduciary duty of "loyalty" requires the agent to put the client's interests above all others, including their own.

➡23. What is the term for an agent who represents both the buyer and the seller in the same transaction?

A. Single agent

B. Dual agent

C. Sub-agent

D. Transaction broker

Answer: B

An agent who represents both the buyer and the seller in the same transaction is known as a dual agent.

➡24. What is the fiduciary duty of "reasonable care and diligence" concerned with?

A. Protecting the client's financial interests

B. Disclosing all material facts

C. Keeping all information confidential

D. Following all of the client's instructions

Answer: A

The fiduciary duty of "reasonable care and diligence" requires the agent to protect the client's financial interests in the transaction.

➡**25. What is the term for a written agreement between the agent and the client?**

A. Listing agreement

B. Agency agreement

C. Contract

D. Memorandum of understanding

Answer: B

A written agreement between the agent and the client outlining the scope of their relationship is known as an agency agreement.

➡**26. What is the primary purpose of a seller's agent?**

A. To represent the buyer

B. To represent the seller

C. To market the property

D. To negotiate the best price for themselves

Answer: B

The primary purpose of a seller's agent is to represent the seller's interests in the transaction.

➡**27. What is the fiduciary duty of "confidentiality" concerned with?**

A. Protecting the client's financial interests

B. Disclosing all material facts

C. Keeping all information confidential

D. Following all of the client's instructions

Answer: C

The fiduciary duty of "confidentiality" requires the agent to keep all client information confidential unless required to disclose it by law.

➡28. What is the term for an agent who does not represent either party and simply facilitates the transaction?

A. Single agent

B. Dual agent

C. Transaction broker

D. Sub-agent

Answer: C

An agent who does not represent either party and simply facilitates the transaction is known as a transaction broker.

➡29. What is the primary purpose of a dual agent?

A. To represent the buyer

B. To represent the seller

C. To represent both the buyer and the seller

D. To market the property

Answer: C

The primary purpose of a dual agent is to represent both the buyer and the seller in the same transaction.

➡30. What is the fiduciary duty of "full disclosure" concerned with?

A. Protecting the client's financial interests

B. Disclosing all material facts

C. Keeping all information confidential

D. Following all of the client's instructions

Answer: B

The fiduciary duty of "full disclosure" requires the agent to disclose all material facts that could affect the client's decisions.

➡31. What is the term for an agent who represents the buyer exclusively?

A. Buyer's agent

B. Seller's agent

C. Dual agent

D. Transaction broker

Answer: A

A buyer's agent exclusively represents the buyer's interests in a real estate transaction.

➡32. What is the term used to describe the agent's responsibility to act in the best interests of the client?

A. Loyalty

B. Obedience

C. Disclosure

D. Confidentiality

Answer: A

The term "loyalty" is used to describe the agent's fiduciary duty to act in the best interests of the client.

➡33. What is the legal obligation called when an agent must keep the client's information confidential even after the agency relationship has ended?

   A. Perpetual confidentiality
   B. Eternal secrecy
   C. Ongoing disclosure
   D. Extended loyalty

Answer: A

The legal obligation is called "perpetual confidentiality," requiring the agent to keep the client's information confidential indefinitely, even after the agency relationship has ended.

➡34. What does the fiduciary duty of "accounting" require?

   A. Keeping accurate financial records
   B. Disclosing all material facts
   C. Keeping all information confidential
   D. Following all of the client's instructions

Answer: A

The fiduciary duty of "accounting" requires the agent to keep accurate financial records related to the transaction.

➡35. What is the term for a written agreement between a buyer and an agent?

   A. Buyer's agreement
   B. Listing agreement
   C. Agency agreement
   D. Purchase agreement

Answer: A

A written agreement between a buyer and an agent is known as a buyer's agreement.

➡36. What is the primary purpose of a listing agent?

  A. To represent the buyer
  B. To represent the seller
  C. To market the property
  D. To negotiate the best price for themselves

Answer: C

The primary purpose of a listing agent is to market the property to potential buyers.

➡37. What is the fiduciary duty of "disclosure" concerned with?

  A. Protecting the client's financial interests
  B. Disclosing all material facts
  C. Keeping all information confidential
  D. Following all of the client's instructions

Answer: B

The fiduciary duty of "disclosure" requires the agent to disclose all material facts that could affect the client's decisions.

➡38. What is the term for an agent who represents the seller exclusively?

  A. Buyer's agent
  B. Seller's agent
  C. Dual agent
  D. Transaction broker

Answer: B

A seller's agent exclusively represents the seller's interests in a real estate transaction.

➡39. What is the primary role of a dual agent?

    A. To represent the buyer

    B. To represent the seller

    C. To represent both the buyer and the seller

    D. To market the property

Answer: C

The primary role of a dual agent is to represent both the buyer and the seller in the same transaction.

➡40. What is the fiduciary duty of "loyalty" concerned with?

    A. Protecting the client's financial interests

    B. Disclosing all material facts

    C. Keeping all information confidential

    D. Putting the client's interests above all others

Answer: D

The fiduciary duty of "loyalty" requires the agent to put the client's interests above all others, including their own.

➡41. What is the primary purpose of a buyer's agent in a real estate transaction?

    A. To represent the seller's interests

    B. To represent the buyer's interests

    C. To act as a neutral third party

    D. To facilitate the transaction without representation

Answer: B

The primary purpose of a buyer's agent is to represent the interests of the buyer in a real estate transaction.

➡42. What is the fiduciary duty that requires an agent to be honest and forthright with the client?

A. Loyalty

B. Disclosure

C. Obedience

D. Accountability

Answer: B

The fiduciary duty of disclosure requires an agent to be honest and forthright with the client, providing all relevant information.

➡43. What is the term for the legal relationship between a principal and an agent where the agent is expected to represent the principal's interests?

A. Contractual agreement

B. Fiduciary relationship

C. Business partnership

D. Legal guardianship

Answer: B

The term "fiduciary relationship" describes the legal relationship between a principal and an agent, where the agent is expected to represent the principal's interests with the utmost good faith, trust, confidence, and candor.

➡44. What is the fiduciary duty that requires an agent to follow all lawful instructions from the client?

A. Obedience

B. Loyalty

C. Disclosure

D. Accountability

Answer: A
The fiduciary duty of obedience requires an agent to follow all lawful instructions given by the client.

➟**45. What is the term used to describe the agent's responsibility to safeguard the client's financial interests?**

  A. Accountability
  B. Loyalty
  C. Disclosure
  D. Obedience

Answer: A
The term "accountability" is used to describe the agent's fiduciary duty to safeguard the client's financial interests.

➟**46. What is the legal obligation called when an agent must disclose any known defects of the property?**

  A. Material fact disclosure
  B. Defect revelation
  C. Condition reporting
  D. Property transparency

Answer: A
The legal obligation is called "material fact disclosure," requiring the agent to disclose any known defects of the property to the client.

➡47. What is the term used to describe the agent's responsibility to keep the client informed at all times?

A. Loyalty

B. Disclosure

C. Obedience

D. Accountability

Answer: B

The term "disclosure" is used to describe the agent's fiduciary duty to keep the client informed at all times.

➡48. In a dual agency relationship, what must the agent do to avoid conflicts of interest?

A. Represent only the buyer's interests

B. Represent only the seller's interests

C. Obtain written consent from both parties

D. Avoid disclosing any confidential information to either party

Answer: C

In a dual agency relationship, the agent must obtain written consent from both parties to avoid conflicts of interest. This ensures that both the buyer and the seller are aware of the situation and agree to it.

➡49. Which of the following is NOT a duty of an agent towards their client?

A. Confidentiality

B. Obedience

C. Disclosure

D. Independence

Answer: D

Independence is not a duty of an agent towards their client. Agents are expected to act in the best interests of their clients, which includes duties like confidentiality, obedience, and disclosure.

➡️50. What is the term for a situation where an agent represents both the buyer and the seller in a transaction?

   A. Double agency
   B. Single agency
   C. Sub-agency
   D. Non-agency

Answer: A

The term for a situation where an agent represents both the buyer and the seller in a transaction is called "double agency." This situation requires informed consent from both parties and can present a conflict of interest for the agent.

Property Valuation and Financial Analysis

Understanding property valuation and financial analysis is not just a skill but an art that every real estate professional must master. In Washington State, where the real estate market is known for its dynamic and sometimes volatile nature, these skills are even more critical. This chapter aims to provide a comprehensive guide to property valuation and financial analysis, focusing on the unique aspects of Washington State's real estate market.

The Importance of Accurate Property Valuation

Why Accurate Valuation Matters

Accurate property valuation is the cornerstone of any real estate transaction. For sellers, it helps in setting a competitive yet profitable listing price. For buyers, it serves as a tool for negotiating a fair purchase price. For agents, it's a critical skill that can significantly impact their success and reputation. In Washington, where property prices can vary significantly even within the same neighborhood, an accurate valuation is crucial.

Comparative Market Analysis (CMA)

What is CMA?

One of the most common methods for valuing residential property is Comparative Market Analysis (CMA). This involves comparing the property in question to similar properties that have recently sold, are currently on the market, or were listed but did not sell.

How to Conduct a CMA

Conducting a CMA involves several steps. First, you'll need to identify comparable properties, or "comps," which are similar in size, location, condition, and features. Then, you'll need to adjust for differences between the comps and your property. Finally, you'll analyze the data to arrive at a valuation.

CMA in Washington State

In Washington State, the CMA process can be more complex due to the state's diverse range of property types and market conditions. For example, a CMA for a waterfront property in Seattle would be vastly different from one for a rural property in Eastern Washington.

Appraisal

What is an Appraisal?

While CMA is often sufficient for most transactions, some situations—like complex estates or commercial properties—may require a formal appraisal. An appraisal is a more detailed and systematic process conducted by a licensed appraiser.

Appraisal Process

The appraisal process involves a thorough inspection of the property, an analysis of the local market, and a review of comparable sales. The appraiser may also use other valuation methods, such as the income approach for rental properties or the cost approach for new constructions.

Appraisal in Washington State

In Washington State, only licensed appraisers can conduct formal appraisals. The state has specific guidelines and criteria that appraisers must follow, making their evaluations highly reliable but also more costly than a CMA.

Financial Analysis: Beyond the Listing Price

Return on Investment (ROI)

What is ROI?

Return on Investment (ROI) is a key metric used to evaluate the profitability of an investment property. It's calculated by dividing the net profit of the investment by the initial cost and is usually expressed as a percentage.

Calculating ROI

The formula for ROI is simple: (Net Profit / Cost of Investment) x 100 = ROI%. However, calculating the net profit and cost of investment can be complex, involving various expenses and revenues.

ROI in Washington State

In Washington State, where property values have been historically strong, understanding ROI can help investors make informed decisions. The state offers various opportunities for high ROI, but it's crucial to consider factors like location, property type, and market trends.

Cash Flow Analysis

What is Cash Flow?

Cash flow is the net amount of money moving in and out of your investment. For rental properties, this involves calculating the monthly income generated by the property and subtracting all expenses, including mortgage payments, maintenance, and taxes.

Calculating Cash Flow

To calculate cash flow, you'll need to consider various income streams and expenses. Income can include rent, parking fees, and other ancillary revenue, while expenses can range from mortgage payments to property management fees.

Cash Flow in Washington State

Washington State offers various opportunities for positive cash flow, especially in growing markets like Seattle, Tacoma, and Spokane. However, high property taxes and maintenance costs can impact cash flow, making it crucial to conduct a thorough financial analysis.

Tax Implications

Federal Taxes

Real estate investments are subject to various federal taxes, including income tax on rental income and capital gains tax on property sales. However, there are also various deductions and tax benefits available to property owners.

Washington State Taxes

Washington State has specific tax laws related to real estate that can impact your financial analysis. For instance, there's no personal income tax, but there are property taxes and a real estate excise tax to consider.

Tax Planning

Effective tax planning can significantly impact the profitability of your real estate investment. This involves understanding the various deductions, credits, and tax benefits available to you and planning your investment strategy accordingly.

Advanced Valuation Methods

Income Capitalization Approach

This method is particularly useful for properties that generate income. It involves calculating the present value of future income streams generated by the property. This is a common approach for valuing commercial properties and larger residential buildings.

Cost Approach

This involves calculating how much it would cost to replace the property, considering both the value of the land and the cost of construction. This method is often used for unique or specialized properties where comparable sales data is not available.

Conclusion

Property valuation and financial analysis are complex but essential aspects of real estate transactions in Washington State. Whether you're a seasoned investor or a first-time homebuyer, understanding these principles can help you make informed decisions and maximize your financial gains. From Comparative Market Analysis to advanced valuation methods, and from ROI calculations to tax implications, each element plays a crucial role in the real estate landscape of Washington State.

Mock Exam Property Valuation and Financial Analysis

➡1. Which property valuation method is most commonly used for residential properties?

    A. Sales Comparison Approach

    B. Cost Approach

    C. Income Approach

    D. ROI Method

Answer: A. Sales Comparison Approach

The Sales Comparison Approach is most commonly used for residential properties. It involves comparing the property to similar ones that have recently sold.

➡2. What does ROI stand for in real estate financial analysis?

    A. Return On Investment

    B. Rate Of Interest

    C. Real Estate Opportunity Index

    D. Return On Infrastructure

Answer: A. Return On Investment

ROI stands for Return On Investment. It's a key metric used to evaluate the profitability of an investment property.

➡3. What is the Debt Service Coverage Ratio (DSCR) used for?

    A. Calculating property taxes

    B. Assessing a property's ability to cover its debt obligations

    C. Determining the property's market value

    D. Calculating the monthly rent

Answer: B. Assessing a property's ability to cover its debt obligations

DSCR is used to assess a property's ability to cover its debt obligations. A DSCR greater than 1 indicates that the property is generating sufficient income to cover its debts.

➡️4. Which of the following factors does NOT affect property valuation?

A. Location

B. Size and Layout

C. Color of the walls

D. Market Conditions

Answer: C. Color of the walls

The color of the walls is generally not a significant factor affecting property valuation. Location, size, and market conditions are more impactful.

➡️5. What is Cash Flow Analysis used for in real estate?

A. Calculating monthly income and expenses

B. Assessing property taxes

C. Determining market value

D. Calculating ROI

Answer: A. Calculating monthly income and expenses

Cash Flow Analysis is used to calculate the monthly income generated by the property, subtracting all expenses, to determine the net cash flow.

➡️6. What does a DSCR of less than 1 indicate?

A. The property is generating sufficient income

B. The property is not generating enough income to cover debts

C. The property is overvalued

D. The property is undervalued

Answer: B. The property is not generating enough income to cover debts**

A DSCR of less than 1 indicates that the property is not generating sufficient income to cover its debt obligations.

➡7. In the Sales Comparison Approach, what is adjusted for when comparing properties?

  A. Only the size
  B. Only the location
  C. Features, location, and other factors
  D. Only the features

Answer: C. Features, location, and other factors

Explanation: In the Sales Comparison Approach, adjustments are made for differences in features, location, and other factors to make a fair comparison.

➡8. What is the Cost Approach commonly used for?

  A. Old properties
  B. New properties
  C. Commercial properties
  D. Rental properties

Answer: B. New properties

Explanation: The Cost Approach is often used for new properties. It involves calculating how much it would cost to replace the property, then adjusting for depreciation and land value.

➡9. Which of the following is NOT a financial analysis tool in real estate?

  A. ROI
  B. DSCR

C. Cash Flow Analysis

D. Gross Domestic Product (GDP)

Answer: D. Gross Domestic Product (GDP)

GDP is not a financial analysis tool used in real estate. ROI, DSCR, and Cash Flow Analysis are commonly used metrics.

➡10. What is the Income Approach commonly used for?

A. Residential properties

B. Commercial properties

C. New properties

D. Old properties

Answer: B. Commercial properties

The Income Approach is commonly used for commercial properties. It involves calculating the present value of future cash flows the property is expected to generate.

➡11. What does the term 'amortization' refer to in real estate?

A. The process of increasing property value

B. The gradual reduction of a loan balance through regular payments

C. The increase in property tax over time

D. The depreciation of property value due to age

Answer: B. The gradual reduction of a loan balance through regular payments

Amortization refers to the gradual reduction of a loan balance through regular payments over time.

➡12. What is the primary focus of a Comparative Market Analysis (CMA)?

A. To compare the ROI of different properties

B. To assess the fair market value of a property

C. To evaluate the debt service coverage ratio

D. To calculate the net operating income

Answer: B. To assess the fair market value of a property

A Comparative Market Analysis (CMA) is primarily used to assess the fair market value of a property by comparing it to similar properties that have recently sold or are currently on the market.

➡️**13. What does LTV stand for in real estate?**

    A. Loan To Value

    B. Long Term Viability

    C. Lease To Vendor

    D. Land Transfer Value

Answer: A. Loan To Value

LTV stands for Loan To Value, which is a ratio that compares the amount of a loan to the value of the property being purchased.

➡️**14. What is the primary purpose of a cap rate in real estate?**

    A. To measure the risk associated with a property

    B. To calculate the monthly mortgage payment

    C. To determine the property tax rate

    D. To assess the age of the property

Answer: A. To measure the risk associated with a property

The cap rate, or capitalization rate, is used to measure the risk associated with a property and its potential return on investment.

➡️**15. What is the formula for calculating Net Operating Income (NOI)?**

A. Gross Income - Operating Expenses

B. Gross Income + Operating Expenses

C. (Gross Income - Operating Expenses) / Gross Income

D. Operating Expenses - Gross Income

Answer: A. Gross Income - Operating Expenses

Net Operating Income (NOI) is calculated by subtracting operating expenses from the gross income generated by the property.

➡️**16. What is the Debt Service Coverage Ratio (DSCR) primarily used for?**

A. To determine the profitability of a property

B. To assess a borrower's ability to cover loan payments

C. To calculate property taxes

D. To evaluate the market value of a property

Answer: B. To assess a borrower's ability to cover loan payments

DSCR is used to evaluate a borrower's ability to cover loan payments from the property's net operating income.

➡️**17. What does the Gross Rent Multiplier (GRM) measure?**

A. The property's operating expenses

B. The property's potential for appreciation

C. The property's value relative to its gross rental income

D. The property's maintenance costs

Answer: C. The property's value relative to its gross rental income

GRM measures the property's value in relation to its gross rental income.

➡️**18. What is the primary purpose of a 'due diligence' period in real estate transactions?**

A. To secure financing

B. To conduct inspections and verify property details

C. To negotiate the price

D. To find tenants

Answer: B. To conduct inspections and verify property details

The due diligence period allows the buyer to conduct inspections and verify property details before finalizing the purchase.

➡19. What does the term 'equity' refer to in real estate?

A. The market value of a property

B. The difference between the property's market value and the outstanding loan amount

C. The annual rental income

D. The initial down payment

Answer: B. The difference between the property's market value and the outstanding loan amount

Equity is the difference between the market value of the property and the amount still owed on any loans.

➡20. What is a 'contingency' in a real estate contract?

A. A binding agreement

B. A penalty for late payment

C. A condition that must be met for the contract to proceed

D. An optional add-on to the contract

Answer: C. A condition that must be met for the contract to proceed

A contingency is a condition or action that must be met for a real estate contract to become binding.

➡21. What is the primary advantage of a 'fixed-rate mortgage'?

    A. Lower initial payments

    B. Flexibility in payment amounts

    C. Interest rate remains constant

    D. No down payment required

Answer: C. Interest rate remains constant

The main advantage of a fixed-rate mortgage is that the interest rate remains constant over the life of the loan.

➡22. What is the 'appraisal' primarily used for in real estate?

    A. To assess property taxes

    B. To determine the market value of a property

    C. To calculate the ROI

    D. To evaluate the property's condition

Answer: B. To determine the market value of a property

An appraisal is primarily used to determine the market value of a property, often for lending purposes.

➡23. What does 'underwriting' refer to in the context of real estate financing?

    A. The process of verifying loan documents

    B. The process of evaluating a borrower's creditworthiness

    C. The drafting of the mortgage contract

    D. The calculation of interest rates

Answer: B. The process of evaluating a borrower's creditworthiness

Underwriting refers to the process where a lender evaluates the creditworthiness of a potential borrower.

➡24. What is 'cash flow' in the context of real estate investment?

   A. The total value of the property

   B. The money generated after all expenses are paid

   C. The initial investment amount

   D. The annual property tax

Answer: B. The money generated after all expenses are paid

Cash flow is the money left over after all expenses, including mortgage payments and maintenance, are paid.

➡25. What does 'closing costs' include in a real estate transaction?

   A. Only the down payment

   B. Only the broker's commission

   C. Various fees like loan origination, appraisal, and legal fees

   D. Only property taxes

Answer: C. Various fees like loan origination, appraisal, and legal fees

Closing costs include a variety of fees such as loan origination fees, appraisal fees, and legal fees, among others.

➡26. What is the primary purpose of a 'cap rate' in real estate investment?

   A. To measure the risk associated with the property

   B. To calculate the property taxes

   C. To determine the mortgage interest rate

   D. To assess the property's condition

Answer: A. To measure the risk associated with the property

The cap rate is used to measure the risk and potential return of a real estate investment.

➡27. What does 'amortization' refer to in a mortgage context?

A. The process of increasing property value

B. The process of paying off debt over time

C. The initial down payment

D. The annual property tax

Answer: B. The process of paying off debt over time

Amortization refers to the gradual reduction of a debt over a specified period.

➡28. What is a 'balloon mortgage'?

A. A mortgage with no down payment

B. A mortgage with a large final payment

C. A mortgage with fluctuating interest rates

D. A mortgage paid off in two years

Answer: B. A mortgage with a large final payment

A balloon mortgage requires a large lump-sum payment at the end of the loan term.

➡29. What does 'leverage' mean in real estate investment?

A. Using borrowed funds for investment

B. Increasing the property's value through improvements

C. The ratio of debt to equity

D. The annual rental income

Answer: A. Using borrowed funds for investment

Leverage refers to the use of borrowed funds to finance a real estate investment.

➡30. What is 'escrow' in a real estate transaction?

A. A legal agreement between buyer and seller

B. An account where funds are held until the transaction is completed

C. The commission paid to the real estate agent

D. The initial offer made by the buyer

Answer: B. An account where funds are held until the transaction is completed

Escrow is an account where funds are held by a third party until specific conditions are met.

➡ **31. What is the 'loan-to-value ratio' used for?**

A. To determine the interest rate

B. To calculate the down payment

C. To assess the risk of the loan

D. To measure property appreciation

Answer: C. To assess the risk of the loan

The loan-to-value ratio is used by lenders to evaluate the risk associated with a mortgage loan.

➡ **32. What does 'negative gearing' refer to in real estate investment?**

A. When rental income exceeds expenses

B. When expenses exceed rental income

C. When the property value decreases

D. When the mortgage is paid off

Answer: B. When expenses exceed rental income

Negative gearing occurs when the costs of owning a property exceed the income it generates.

➡ **33. What is a '1031 exchange'?**

A. A tax-deferred property exchange

B. A type of mortgage

C. A property valuation method

D. A type of property insurance

Answer: A. A tax-deferred property exchange

A 1031 exchange allows the owner to sell a property and reinvest the proceeds in a new property while deferring capital gains tax.

➥**34. What is 'equity' in a property?**

A. The market value of the property

B. The amount owed on the mortgage

C. The property's purchase price

D. The difference between the property's value and the mortgage balance

Answer: D. The difference between the property's value and the mortgage balance

Equity is the value of ownership interest in the property, calculated as the property's market value minus the remaining mortgage balance.

➥**35. What does 'due diligence' mean in a real estate context?**

A. The initial deposit made by the buyer

B. The research and analysis done before purchasing a property

C. The final inspection of the property

D. The negotiation process between buyer and seller

Answer: B. The research and analysis done before purchasing a property

Due diligence refers to the comprehensive appraisal and verification of a property before buying it.

➥**36. What is a 'second mortgage'?**

A. A mortgage taken out on a second property

B. A mortgage that replaces the first one

C. An additional loan secured by the same property

D. A mortgage with a second lender

Answer: C. An additional loan secured by the same property

A second mortgage is a loan that is secured by the equity in your home, in addition to your primary mortgage.

➡37. What is 'imputed rent'?

A. Rent paid in advance

B. The rental value of a property you own and live in

C. Rent paid in installments

D. The tax on rental income

Answer: B. The rental value of a property you own and live in

Imputed rent is the economic theory of the rent you could be earning from leasing a property instead of living in it.

➡38. What is a 'fixed-rate mortgage'?

A. A mortgage with fluctuating interest rates

B. A mortgage with a constant interest rate

C. A mortgage with a variable down payment

D. A mortgage that can be paid off at any time

Answer: B. A mortgage with a constant interest rate

A fixed-rate mortgage has an interest rate that remains the same for the entire term of the loan.

➡39. What is 'redlining'?

A. A method of property valuation

B. Discriminatory practice in lending or insurance

C. A type of property insurance

D. A method of calculating mortgage interest

Answer: B. Discriminatory practice in lending or insurance

Redlining is an unethical practice where services are denied or priced differently in certain areas, often based on racial or ethnic composition.

➡**40. What is 'gross yield' in real estate investment?**

A. Annual rent divided by property value

B. Monthly rent multiplied by 12

C. Property value divided by annual rent

D. Annual rent minus expenses

Answer: A. Annual rent divided by property value

Gross yield is calculated by taking the annual rental income, dividing it by the property value, and then multiplying by 100 to get a percentage.

➡**41. What does 'amortization' refer to in a mortgage context?**

A. The process of increasing property value

B. The process of paying off debt over time

C. The process of calculating interest rates

D. The process of transferring property ownership

Answer: B. The process of paying off debt over time

Amortization refers to the gradual reduction of a debt over a given period.

➡**42. What is a 'balloon payment'?**

A. A small initial down payment

B. A large final payment at the end of a loan term

C. A monthly mortgage payment

D. An extra payment to reduce loan principal

Answer: B. A large final payment at the end of a loan term

A balloon payment is a large, lump-sum payment made at the end of a loan's term.

➠**43. What is 'capital gains tax'?**

A. Tax on rental income

B. Tax on the sale of a property

C. Tax on property purchase

D. Tax on mortgage interest

Answer: B. Tax on the sale of a property

Capital gains tax is levied on the profit made from selling a property.

➠**44. What is a 'contingency' in a real estate contract?**

A. A penalty clause

B. A condition that must be met for the contract to proceed

C. A fixed closing date

D. A mandatory down payment

Answer: B. A condition that must be met for the contract to proceed

A contingency is a condition or action that must be met for a real estate contract to become binding.

➠**45. What is 'escrow'?**

A. A type of mortgage

B. A legal arrangement where a third party holds assets

C. A method of property valuation

D. A type of property insurance

Answer: B. A legal arrangement where a third party holds assets

Escrow is a legal concept where a financial instrument or asset is held by a third party on behalf of two other parties in a transaction.

➡ **46. What is 'net operating income' in real estate?**

A. Gross income minus expenses

B. Gross income plus expenses

C. Property value minus mortgage

D. Annual rent divided by property value

Answer: A. Gross income minus expenses

Net operating income is the total income generated by a property, minus the operating expenses.

➡ **47. What does 'underwriting' refer to in real estate?**

A. The process of property valuation

B. The process of assessing the risk of a loan

C. The process of property inspection

D. The process of transferring property ownership

Answer: B. The process of assessing the risk of a loan

Underwriting is the process by which a lender evaluates the risk of offering a mortgage loan.

➡ **48. What is 'zoning' in real estate?**

A. The process of property valuation

B. The division of land into areas for specific uses

C. The process of property inspection

D. The process of transferring property ownership

Answer: B. The division of land into areas for specific uses

Zoning refers to municipal or local laws or regulations that dictate how real property can and cannot be used in certain areas.

➡️**49. What is 'leverage' in real estate investment?**

A. Using borrowed funds for investment

B. The ratio of debt to equity

C. The process of property valuation

D. The process of property inspection

Answer: A. Using borrowed funds for investment

Leverage in real estate refers to using borrowed capital for the purpose of expanding the potential return of an investment.

➡️**50. What is a 'real estate bubble'?**

A. A period of rapid increase in property value

B. A period of rapid decrease in property value

C. A stable real estate market

D. A period of high rental income

Answer: A. A period of rapid increase in property value

A real estate bubble refers to a period of speculative excess where property prices rise rapidly and unsustainably.

Financing

Financing is a cornerstone of real estate transactions, and understanding its intricacies is crucial for anyone involved in buying or selling property. In Washington State, where the real estate market is both dynamic and competitive, securing the right type of financing can make all the difference. This chapter aims to provide a comprehensive guide to financing options, processes, and best practices specific to Washington State's real estate market.

The Mortgage Landscape in Washington State

Conventional Mortgages

What Are They?

Conventional mortgages are loans that are not insured by the federal government. They are the most common type of mortgage and come in various forms, including fixed-rate and adjustable-rate mortgages.

Requirements

To qualify for a conventional mortgage in Washington State, you'll generally need a credit score of at least 620 and a down payment of 5-20%. Lenders will also look at your debt-to-income ratio and employment history.

Government-Backed Mortgages

FHA Loans

Federal Housing Administration (FHA) loans are popular among first-time homebuyers because they require a lower down payment (as low as 3.5%) and have more lenient credit requirements.

VA Loans

Veterans Affairs (VA) loans are available to veterans and active-duty military personnel. These loans require no down payment and no private mortgage insurance (PMI), making them an excellent option for eligible individuals.

USDA Loans

The U.S. Department of Agriculture (USDA) offers loans for rural properties. While not as common in Washington State's urban areas like Seattle, they are an option in more rural parts of the state.

The Loan Application Process

Pre-Approval

Importance

Getting pre-approved for a mortgage gives you an idea of how much you can afford and shows sellers that you are a serious buyer. In Washington's competitive market, a pre-approval letter can give you an edge.

Steps to Get Pre-Approved

Credit Check: The lender will perform a credit check to assess your creditworthiness.
Documentation: You'll need to provide various documents, including proof of income, employment verification, and financial statements.
Loan Estimate: After assessing your financial situation, the lender will provide a loan estimate, which will give you an idea of the loan amount, interest rate, and other terms you might qualify for.

Loan Application

Once you've found a property and have a purchase agreement, the next step is to complete the loan application. This involves providing additional documentation and choosing your loan type.

Underwriting

The underwriting process involves a detailed examination of your financial situation, property appraisal, and other factors. The underwriter will then approve, deny, or request additional information for the loan.

Closing

The closing process involves signing all the loan documents, including the loan agreement and mortgage note. You'll also pay any closing costs and the down payment at this time.

Interest Rates and APR

Understanding Interest Rates

The interest rate is the cost of borrowing the principal loan amount. It can be fixed or variable, depending on the type of loan you choose.

What is APR?

The Annual Percentage Rate (APR) includes the interest rate and other loan costs, providing a more complete picture of the loan's total cost.

Interest Rates in Washington State

Interest rates can vary widely in Washington State due to factors like loan type, borrower's credit score, and economic conditions. It's crucial to shop around and compare rates from different lenders.

Down Payments and PMI

Down Payment Requirements

The down payment is a percentage of the property's purchase price that you pay upfront. While many conventional loans require a 20% down payment, government-backed loans like FHA and VA loans have lower requirements.

Private Mortgage Insurance (PMI)

If your down payment is less than 20%, you'll likely have to pay Private Mortgage Insurance (PMI). This is an additional cost that protects the lender if you default on the loan.

Special Financing Programs in Washington State

First-Time Homebuyer Programs

Washington State offers several programs to assist first-time homebuyers, including down payment assistance and reduced interest rates.

Washington State Housing Finance Commission (WSHFC)

The WSHFC offers various loan programs and resources for low- and moderate-income families, including down payment assistance and homebuyer education.

Conclusion

Financing is a complex but crucial aspect of real estate transactions in Washington State. Whether you're a first-time homebuyer or a seasoned investor, understanding the types of loans available, the application and approval process, and the financial implications can help you make informed decisions. From conventional and government-backed loans to special state programs, each financing option comes with its own set of requirements, benefits, and drawbacks. By understanding these intricacies, you can navigate Washington State's dynamic real estate market more effectively.

Mock Exam Financing

➡1. What is the minimum down payment generally required for a conventional loan?

   A. 3.5%

   B. 5%

   C. 10%

   D. 20%

Answer: D. 20%

Conventional loans usually require a higher down payment, often 20%, to avoid the need for mortgage insurance.

➡2. Which type of loan is backed by the Federal Housing Administration?

   A. Conventional Loan

   B. FHA Loan

   C. VA Loan

   D. ARM

Answer: B. FHA Loan

FHA loans are backed by the Federal Housing Administration and are designed for low-to-moderate-income borrowers.

➡3. Who is eligible for a VA loan?

   A. First-time homebuyers

   B. Veterans and active-duty military personnel

   C. Low-income borrowers

   D. Investors

Answer: B. Veterans and active-duty military personnel

VA loans are a benefit specifically for veterans and active-duty military personnel.

➡ 4. What is the main feature of an Adjustable-Rate Mortgage (ARM)?

A. Fixed interest rate

B. Lower initial interest rate

C. No down payment

D. Easier credit requirements

Answer: B. Lower initial interest rate

ARMs often start with lower rates than fixed-rate mortgages but the rates can increase over time.

➡ 5. What do interest-only loans allow you to pay initially?

A. Only the principal

B. Only the interest

C. Both principal and interest

D. Down payment only

Answer: B. Only the interest

Interest-only loans allow you to pay just the interest for a specific initial period, usually 5-10 years.

➡ 6. What is the first step in the mortgage process?

A. Loan Application

B. Pre-Approval

C. Underwriting

D. Closing

Answer: B. Pre-Approval

Before looking at properties, it's advisable to get pre-approved for a mortgage, which involves a lender checking your financial background.

➠7. What does the underwriting process involve?

   A. Property inspection
   B. Financial due diligence
   C. Property selection
   D. Loan repayment

Answer: B. Financial due diligence

During underwriting, the lender assesses your financial situation in detail and checks the property appraisal.

➠8. What is usually included in closing costs?

   A. Monthly mortgage payments
   B. Down payment
   C. Loan origination fees
   D. Property taxes

Answer: C. Loan origination fees

Closing costs can include loan origination fees, appraisal fees, title searches, and more.

➠9. What can significantly impact your monthly mortgage payments?

   A. Type of property
   B. Real estate agent's commission
   C. Interest rates
   D. Home inspection fees

Answer: C. Interest rates

The interest rate on your mortgage will significantly impact your monthly payments and the overall cost of the loan.

➡10. What is often included in monthly mortgage payments and paid by the lender annually?

  A. Closing costs
  B. Down payment
  C. Property taxes and homeowner's insurance
  D. Mortgage insurance

Answer: C. Property taxes and homeowner's insurance

Property taxes and homeowner's insurance are often included in monthly mortgage payments and are then paid by the lender on an annual basis.

➡11. What is the purpose of a good faith estimate?

  A. To provide an estimate of closing costs
  B. To lock in an interest rate
  C. To guarantee loan approval
  D. To assess property value

Answer: A. To provide an estimate of closing costs

A good faith estimate is provided by the lender to give you an idea of your closing costs.

➡12. What is a balloon mortgage?

  A. A mortgage with fluctuating interest rates
  B. A mortgage that requires a large payment at the end
  C. A mortgage with no down payment
  D. A mortgage with very low monthly payments

Answer: B. A mortgage that requires a large payment at the end

A balloon mortgage requires a large lump sum payment at the end of the loan term.

➡13. What does LTV stand for?

A. Loan To Value

B. Long Term Viability

C. Loan Transfer Variable

D. Low Transaction Volume

Answer: A. Loan To Value

LTV stands for Loan To Value, which is the ratio of the loan amount to the value of the property.

➡14. What is a home equity loan?

A. A loan for first-time homebuyers

B. A loan based on the value of your home

C. A loan for home repairs

D. A loan for investment properties

Answer: B. A loan based on the value of your home

A home equity loan is a type of loan where the borrower uses the equity of their home as collateral.

➡15. What is PMI?

A. Property Management Insurance

B. Private Mortgage Insurance

C. Public Mortgage Index

D. Property Maintenance Inclusion

Answer: B. Private Mortgage Insurance

PMI stands for Private Mortgage Insurance, which is usually required when the down payment is less than 20%.

➡16. What is a reverse mortgage?

A. A mortgage for seniors to convert equity into cash

B. A mortgage with reverse interest rates

C. A mortgage that pays the borrower

D. A mortgage for investment properties

Answer: A. A mortgage for seniors to convert equity into cash

A reverse mortgage allows seniors to convert the equity in their home into cash, usually for living expenses.

➡17. What is the main advantage of a 15-year mortgage over a 30-year mortgage?

A. Lower interest rates

B. Lower monthly payments

C. No down payment

D. No closing costs

Answer: A. Lower interest rates

A 15-year mortgage typically offers lower interest rates and allows you to build equity faster.

➡18. What does refinancing a mortgage mean?

A. Changing the terms of your mortgage

B. Extending your mortgage term

C. Taking out a second mortgage

D. Defaulting on your mortgage

Answer: A. Changing the terms of your mortgage

Refinancing involves replacing your existing mortgage with a new one, usually with better terms.

➡19. What is a credit score primarily used for in the mortgage process?

    A. To determine eligibility for certain types of loans

    B. To decide the size of the down payment

    C. To set the property value

    D. To calculate closing costs

Answer: A. To determine eligibility for certain types of loans

Your credit score is used to determine your eligibility for loans and the interest rate you'll receive.

➡20. What is a jumbo loan?

    A. A loan for small properties

    B. A loan exceeding conforming loan limits

    C. A loan for commercial properties

    D. A loan for mobile homes

Answer: B. A loan exceeding conforming loan limits

A jumbo loan is a mortgage that exceeds the conforming loan limits set by federal agencies.

➡21. What is the primary purpose of an escrow account in a mortgage?

    A. To hold the down payment

    B. To pay property taxes and insurance

    C. To cover repair costs

    D. To pay off the mortgage early

Answer: B. To pay property taxes and insurance

An escrow account is typically used to hold funds for paying property taxes and insurance.

→22. What is an adjustable-rate mortgage (ARM)?

A. A mortgage with a fixed interest rate

B. A mortgage with an interest rate that can change

C. A mortgage with no interest

D. A mortgage for investment properties

Answer: B. A mortgage with an interest rate that can change

An adjustable-rate mortgage has an interest rate that can change periodically depending on market conditions.

→23. What is the debt-to-income ratio?

A. The ratio of your monthly debt payments to your monthly income

B. The ratio of your loan amount to your property value

C. The ratio of your credit score to your income

D. The ratio of your down payment to your loan amount

Answer: A. The ratio of your monthly debt payments to your monthly income

The debt-to-income ratio is used by lenders to assess your ability to manage payments.

→24. What is a pre-qualification in the mortgage process?

A. A binding agreement between you and the lender

B. An estimate of how much you can borrow

C. A guarantee of a loan

D. A final approval for a loan

Answer: B. An estimate of how much you can borrow

Pre-qualification is an initial step that gives you an estimate of how much you may be able to borrow.

➡ **25. What is the main disadvantage of an interest-only mortgage?**

    A. You can't pay off the principal

    B. You pay more interest over time

    C. You can't refinance

    D. You need a large down payment

Answer: B. You pay more interest over time

With an interest-only mortgage, you end up paying more in interest because you're not reducing the principal.

➡ **26. What does APR stand for?**

    A. Annual Property Rate

    B. Annual Percentage Rate

    C. Approved Payment Rate

    D. Average Price Range

Answer: B. Annual Percentage Rate

APR stands for Annual Percentage Rate, which includes the interest rate and other loan costs.

➡ **27. What is a conforming loan?**

    A. A loan that meets federal guidelines

    B. A loan for investment properties

    C. A loan with no down payment

    D. A loan with a variable interest rate

Answer: A. A loan that meets federal guidelines

A conforming loan is one that adheres to the guidelines set by Fannie Mae and Freddie Mac.

➡ 28. What is a VA loan?

  A. A loan for veterans
  B. A loan for vacation homes
  C. A loan for very large properties
  D. A loan for agricultural properties

Answer: A. A loan for veterans

A VA loan is a mortgage loan in the United States guaranteed by the United States Department of Veterans Affairs.

➡ 29. What is the main advantage of a fixed-rate mortgage?

  A. Lower interest rates
  B. Interest rate can decrease
  C. Monthly payments stay the same
  D. No down payment required

Answer: C. Monthly payments stay the same

With a fixed-rate mortgage, your monthly payments are predictable because the interest rate stays the same.

➡ 30. What is underwriting in the context of mortgages?

  A. The process of verifying financial information
  B. The process of selling a mortgage
  C. The process of setting interest rates
  D. The process of inspecting a property

Answer: A. The process of verifying financial information

Underwriting involves verifying your financial information and assessing the risk of offering you a loan.

➡ 31. What is a balloon payment?

    A. A small monthly payment

    B. A large final payment

    C. A payment made annually

    D. A payment made bi-weekly

Answer: B. A large final payment

A balloon payment is a large, lump-sum payment made at the end of a loan term.

➡ 32. What is the purpose of private mortgage insurance (PMI)?

    A. To protect the borrower from foreclosure

    B. To protect the lender if the borrower defaults

    C. To lower the interest rate

    D. To eliminate the need for a down payment

Answer: B. To protect the lender if the borrower defaults

PMI is designed to protect the lender in case the borrower defaults on the loan.

➡ 33. What is the primary purpose of an amortization schedule?

    A. To show the breakdown of each monthly payment into principal and interest

    B. To show the total amount of interest paid over the life of the loan

    C. To show the property's appreciation value over time

    D. To show the borrower's credit score

Answer: A. To show the breakdown of each monthly payment into principal and interest

An amortization schedule provides a detailed breakdown of each monthly payment, showing how much goes toward the principal and how much goes toward interest.

➡34. What is a fixed-rate mortgage?

A. A mortgage with an interest rate that changes over time

B. A mortgage with a constant interest rate for the life of the loan

C. A mortgage with varying monthly payments

D. A mortgage with no interest

Answer: B. A mortgage with a constant interest rate for the life of the loan

A fixed-rate mortgage has an interest rate that remains the same for the entire term of the loan, providing predictability in payments.

➡35. What is a home equity line of credit (HELOC)?

A. A fixed-rate loan

B. A revolving line of credit

C. A type of insurance

D. A government grant

Answer: B. A revolving line of credit

A HELOC is a revolving line of credit that uses your home as collateral.

➡36. What is the loan-to-value ratio (LTV)?

A. The ratio of the loan amount to the property value

B. The ratio of the down payment to the loan amount

C. The ratio of the interest rate to the loan amount

D. The ratio of the loan amount to the borrower's income

Answer: A. The ratio of the loan amount to the property value

The loan-to-value ratio is the amount of the loan compared to the value of the property.

➡ 37. What is a subprime mortgage?

A. A mortgage for borrowers with excellent credit

B. A mortgage for borrowers with poor credit

C. A mortgage with no interest

D. A mortgage for commercial properties

Answer: B. A mortgage for borrowers with poor credit

A subprime mortgage is designed for borrowers who have poor credit history.

➡ 38. What is refinancing?

A. Taking out a second mortgage

B. Replacing an existing loan with a new one

C. Changing the terms of your existing loan

D. Selling your mortgage to another lender

Answer: B. Replacing an existing loan with a new one

Refinancing involves replacing an existing loan with a new one, usually with better terms.

➡ 39. What is a bridge loan?

A. A loan for construction projects

B. A short-term loan to cover the period between two long-term loans

C. A loan for first-time homebuyers

D. A loan for renovating a property

Answer: B. A short-term loan to cover the period between two long-term loans

A bridge loan is a short-term loan used until a person secures permanent financing.

40. What is a seller carry-back?

A. When the seller pays the closing costs

B. When the seller acts as the lender

C. When the seller pays for repairs

D. When the seller pays the agent's commission

Answer: B. When the seller acts as the lender

In a seller carry-back, the seller provides financing to the buyer, essentially acting as the lender.

41. What is the Loan-to-Value (LTV) ratio?

A. The ratio of the loan amount to the property's appraised value

B. The ratio of the loan amount to the borrower's income

C. The ratio of the property's appraised value to the market value

D. The ratio of the down payment to the loan amount

Answer: A. The ratio of the loan amount to the property's appraised value

The Loan-to-Value (LTV) ratio is calculated by dividing the loan amount by the property's appraised value.

42. What does a balloon payment refer to?

A. A large final payment at the end of a loan term

B. Monthly payments that gradually decrease

C. An initial down payment

D. Monthly payments that gradually increase

Answer: A. A large final payment at the end of a loan term

A balloon payment is a large, lump-sum payment made at the end of a loan's term.

➡43. What is the purpose of a "good faith estimate" in mortgage lending?

    A. To provide an estimate of closing costs

    B. To lock in an interest rate

    C. To assess the borrower's creditworthiness

    D. To determine the property's market value

Answer: A. To provide an estimate of closing costs

A "good faith estimate" is provided by the lender to give the borrower an estimate of the closing costs involved in the mortgage process.

➡44. What does the term "amortization" refer to in the context of a mortgage?

    A. The process of increasing the loan amount

    B. The process of paying off the loan over time

    C. The process of adjusting the interest rate

    D. The process of transferring the loan to another lender

Answer: B. The process of paying off the loan over time.

Amortization refers to the process of gradually paying off a loan over a specified period, usually through regular payments that cover both principal and interest.

➡45. What is the primary advantage of a fixed-rate mortgage over an adjustable-rate mortgage?

    A. Lower initial interest rate

    B. Interest rate can decrease over time

    C. Interest rate remains constant over the loan term

    D. Easier qualification criteria

Answer: C. Interest rate remains constant over the loan term

The primary advantage of a fixed-rate mortgage is that the interest rate remains constant over the term of the loan, providing predictability in payments.

➡️46. What is private mortgage insurance (PMI)?

   A. Insurance that protects the lender
   B. Insurance that protects the borrower
   C. Insurance that protects the property
   D. Insurance that protects against natural disasters

Answer: A. Insurance that protects the lender

PMI is insurance that protects the lender in case the borrower defaults on the loan.

➡️47. What is an escrow account primarily used for?

   A. Investing in stocks
   B. Paying property taxes and insurance
   C. Saving for retirement
   D. Paying off the mortgage early

Answer: B. Paying property taxes and insurance

An escrow account is typically used to pay property taxes and insurance premiums.

➡️48. What is a debt-to-income ratio?

   A. The ratio of a borrower's total debt to total income
   B. The ratio of a borrower's credit score to income
   C. The ratio of a borrower's assets to liabilities
   D. The ratio of a borrower's monthly expenses to income

Answer: A. The ratio of a borrower's total debt to total income

The debt-to-income ratio is calculated by dividing a borrower's total debt by their total income.

➡49. What is the primary purpose of a rate lock?

    A. To increase the interest rate over time

    B. To decrease the interest rate over time

    C. To secure an interest rate for a specified period

    D. To allow the interest rate to fluctuate

Answer: C. To secure an interest rate for a specified period

A rate lock secures a specific interest rate for a set period, usually during the loan application process.

➡50. What is a pre-qualification?

    A. A binding agreement between the lender and borrower

    B. An initial assessment of a borrower's creditworthiness

    C. A final approval for a loan

    D. A legal document outlining the terms of the loan

Answer: B. An initial assessment of a borrower's creditworthiness

A pre-qualification is an initial evaluation of a borrower's creditworthiness, usually based on self-reported financial information.

Transfer of Property

The transfer of property is a critical phase in any real estate transaction, and it involves several legal and procedural steps. In Washington State, the process is governed by a set of laws and regulations that aim to protect both the buyer and the seller. This chapter will delve into the intricacies of property transfer, from the initial contract to the final recording of the deed.

The Purchase and Sale Agreement

Overview

The Purchase and Sale Agreement (PSA) is the foundational document that outlines the terms and conditions under which the property will be transferred. It includes details like the purchase price, closing date, and any contingencies that must be met.

Key Elements

Purchase Price: The agreed-upon amount for the property.
Earnest Money: A deposit made by the buyer to show good faith.
Inspection Contingency: Allows the buyer to conduct inspections.
Financing Contingency: Specifies that the buyer must secure financing.
Closing Date: The date by which the transaction must be completed.

Legal Requirements in Washington State

In Washington, the PSA must be in writing to be legally binding. It must also be signed by both parties and include a legal description of the property.

Title Search and Title Insurance

Title Search

A title search is conducted to ensure that the seller has a clear title to the property, meaning there are no liens, encumbrances, or other legal issues that could affect the transfer.

Title Insurance

Title insurance protects the buyer and lender from future claims against the property. In Washington State, it's customary for the seller to pay for the owner's title insurance, while the buyer pays for the lender's title insurance.

The Escrow Process

Role of Escrow

An escrow company acts as a neutral third party to hold funds and documents until all conditions of the PSA are met.

Escrow Instructions

Both parties must provide the escrow company with instructions that outline the steps to be followed for the property transfer.

Closing Costs

Closing costs are fees associated with the transaction, such as loan origination fees, title insurance, and recording fees. In Washington, these are typically split between the buyer and seller, though the exact division can be negotiated.

The Closing

Pre-Closing Steps

Before the closing date, the buyer should conduct a final walk-through of the property to ensure it's in the agreed-upon condition. The lender will also send a Closing Disclosure, summarizing the terms of the loan.

The Closing Meeting

The closing meeting is where all parties sign the necessary documents to finalize the property transfer. These include the deed, the bill of sale, and the settlement statement.

Recording the Deed

After the closing, the deed is recorded with the county recorder's office. This officially transfers the property title from the seller to the buyer.

Special Types of Property Transfer in Washington State

Foreclosures

In the case of foreclosures, the property is sold at a public auction. The highest bidder will receive a Trustee's Deed, transferring ownership.

Short Sales

In a short sale, the lender allows the property to be sold for less than the remaining mortgage balance. This requires lender approval and can be a lengthy process.

Gift Deeds

A gift deed transfers property ownership without any exchange of money. This is common among family members but must be filed and recorded like any other deed.

Tax Implications

Real Estate Excise Tax (REET)

In Washington State, the seller is typically responsible for paying the Real Estate Excise Tax (REET), which is a percentage of the selling price.

Federal Taxes

Both the buyer and seller may have federal tax obligations. For example, the seller may have to pay capital gains tax if the property has appreciated in value.

Conclusion

The transfer of property in Washington State is a multifaceted process that involves various legal and financial steps. From the initial Purchase and Sale Agreement to the final recording of the deed, each stage requires careful attention to detail and adherence to Washington State laws. Whether you're a buyer or a seller, understanding these steps can help you navigate the complexities of property transfer and ensure a smooth, successful transaction.

Mock Exam Transfer of Property

➡1. What is the most common form of voluntary property transfer?

A. Foreclosure

B. Eminent Domain

C. Sales

D. Adverse Possession

Answer: C. Sales

Sales are the most common form of voluntary property transfer, usually involving a straightforward transaction between a buyer and a seller.

➡2. Which type of deed offers the least protection to the buyer?

A. General Warranty Deed

B. Special Warranty Deed

C. Quitclaim Deed

D. Bargain and Sale Deed

Answer: C. Quitclaim Deed

Quitclaim Deeds offer the least protection as they come with no warranties.

➡3. What is the legal process by which a lender can take possession of a property due to default?

A. Eminent Domain

B. Foreclosure

C. Adverse Possession

D. Gifting

Answer: B. Foreclosure

Foreclosure is the legal process that allows a lender to take possession of a property when the owner defaults on mortgage payments.

➡4. What is the minimum requirement for a deed to be enforceable?

A. Oral Agreement

B. Written Instrument

C. Mutual Consent

D. Legal Capacity

Answer: B. Written Instrument

A deed must be in writing to be legally enforceable, complying with state laws.

➡5. What does a Preliminary Title Report outline?

A. Tax implications of the sale

B. Issues with the title

C. Financing options

D. Property valuation

Answer: B. Issues with the title

A Preliminary Title Report outlines any issues with the title that need to be resolved before the sale can proceed.

➡6. What is the purpose of opening an escrow account?

A. To hold funds and documents related to the transaction

B. To pay property taxes

C. To hold the seller's profit

D. To pay the real estate agent's commission

Answer: A. To hold funds and documents related to the transaction

An escrow account is opened to securely hold funds and documents related to the property transaction until all conditions are met.

➠7. What is the term for gaining ownership of a property by occupying it for an extended period under certain conditions?

A. Eminent Domain

B. Foreclosure

C. Adverse Possession

D. Inheritance

Answer: C. Adverse Possession

Adverse Possession allows someone to gain ownership of a property by occupying it for an extended period, provided certain legal conditions are met.

➠8. What type of deed only covers the period of the current owner's tenure?

A. General Warranty Deed

B. Special Warranty Deed

C. Quitclaim Deed

D. Bargain and Sale Deed

Answer: B. Special Warranty Deed

A Special Warranty Deed only covers the period of the current owner's tenure and does not extend back to the property's origins.

➠9. What is the term for the government acquiring private property for public use?

A. Foreclosure

B. Eminent Domain

C. Adverse Possession

D. Gifting

Answer: B. Eminent Domain

Eminent Domain is the legal process by which the government can acquire private property for public use, provided they offer just compensation.

➡10. What is the most common form of consideration in property transfers?

A. Services

B. Money

C. Other assets

D. Promissory notes

Answer: B. Money

Money is the most common form of consideration in property transfers, although other assets or services can also serve this purpose.

➡11. What is the term for a legal claim against a property that must be paid off when the property is sold?

A. Lien

B. Mortgage

C. Easement

D. Covenant

Answer: A. Lien

A lien is a legal claim against a property that must be paid off when the property is sold.

➡12. What is the right to use someone else's land for a specific purpose called?

A. Easement

B. Lien

C. Covenant

D. Mortgage

Answer: A. Easement

An easement grants the right to use another person's land for a specific purpose.

➡ **13. What is the process of dividing a large parcel of land into smaller lots?**

A. Zoning

B. Subdivision

C. Partitioning

D. Rezoning

Answer: B. Subdivision

Subdivision is the process of dividing a larger parcel of land into smaller lots.

➡ **14. What is the term for a restriction on how a property may be used?**

A. Easement

B. Covenant

C. Lien

D. Mortgage

Answer: B. Covenant

A covenant is a restriction on how a property may be used, often found in property deeds or community bylaws.

➡ **15. What is the primary purpose of a title search?**

A. To determine property value

B. To find any restrictions on the property

C. To discover any liens or encumbrances on the property

D. To assess the property's condition

Answer: C. To discover any liens or encumbrances on the property

The primary purpose of a title search is to discover any liens, encumbrances, or other issues that could affect the transfer of property.

➠16. What is the term for the transfer of property upon the owner's death without a will?

A. Probate
B. Intestate
C. Testamentary
D. Inheritance

Answer: B. Intestate

When a property owner dies without a will, the property is transferred according to intestate laws.

➠17. What is the term for a change in property ownership where the new owner assumes the mortgage?

A. Assumption
B. Novation
C. Subletting
D. Foreclosure

Answer: A. Assumption

Assumption is when a new owner takes over the existing mortgage of the property.

➠18. What is the term for the right of a government or its agent to expropriate private property for public use, with payment of compensation?

A. Eminent Domain

B. Foreclosure

C. Adverse Possession

D. Lien

Answer: A. Eminent Domain

Eminent Domain is the right of a government to expropriate private property for public use, with compensation.

⟶19. What is the term for a written document that transfers title of property from one person to another?

A. Mortgage

B. Deed

C. Lien

D. Easement

Answer: B. Deed

A deed is a written document that transfers title of property from one person to another.

⟶20. What is the term for a legal process that involves the distribution of a deceased person's property?

A. Probate

B. Intestate

C. Foreclosure

D. Eminent Domain

Answer: A. Probate

Probate is the legal process involving the distribution of a deceased person's property, especially if they died without a will.

→21. What is the term for acquiring property through the unauthorized occupation of another's land?

   A. Adverse Possession

   B. Eminent Domain

   C. Foreclosure

   D. Probate

Answer: A. Adverse Possession

Adverse Possession is the process of acquiring property by occupying someone else's land without permission for a certain period of time.

→22. What is the term for a legal document that confirms the sale of a property?

   A. Bill of Sale

   B. Deed of Trust

   C. Title Certificate

   D. Warranty Deed

Answer: A. Bill of Sale

A Bill of Sale is a legal document that confirms the sale and transfer of property from one party to another.

→23. What is the term for a legal claim by a lender on the title of a property until a debt is paid off?

   A. Mortgage

   B. Lien

   C. Easement

   D. Covenant

Answer: A. Mortgage

A mortgage is a legal claim by a lender on the title of a property until the debt secured by the mortgage is paid off.

➡️24. What is the term for the legal process by which a lender takes possession of a property due to non-payment?

A. Foreclosure

B. Eminent Domain

C. Probate

D. Adverse Possession

Answer: A. Foreclosure

Foreclosure is the legal process by which a lender takes possession of a property due to the borrower's failure to make required payments.

➡️25. What is the term for a legal agreement that allows one party to use another's property for a specific purpose?

A. Lease

B. Mortgage

C. Easement

D. Lien

Answer: A. Lease

A lease is a legal agreement that allows one party to use another's property for a specific period and for a specific purpose.

➡️26. What is the term for the official document that records the ownership of a property?

A. Title Certificate

B. Bill of Sale

C. Deed of Trust

D. Warranty Deed

Answer: A. Title Certificate

A Title Certificate is the official document that records the ownership of a property.

➡**27. What is the term for a legal restriction on the use of land?**

A. Zoning

B. Easement

C. Mortgage

D. Lien

Answer: A. Zoning

Zoning is a legal restriction that dictates how land in a certain area can be used.

➡**28. What is the term for the right of a property owner to use and enjoy their property without interference?**

A. Quiet Enjoyment

B. Eminent Domain

C. Probate

D. Foreclosure

Answer: A. Quiet Enjoyment

Quiet Enjoyment is the right of a property owner to use and enjoy their property without interference from others.

➡29. What is the term for a legal document that outlines the terms under which a loan will be repaid?

A. Promissory Note

B. Bill of Sale

C. Title Certificate

D. Warranty Deed

Answer: A. Promissory Note

A Promissory Note is a legal document that outlines the terms under which a loan will be repaid.

➡30. What is the term for the legal process of transferring property from a deceased person to their heirs?

A. Inheritance

B. Probate

C. Foreclosure

D. Eminent Domain

Answer: B. Probate

Probate is the legal process of transferring property from a deceased person to their heirs, especially if there is no will.

➡31. What is the term for the legal process that allows the government to take private property for public use?

A. Eminent Domain

B. Foreclosure

C. Adverse Possession

D. Probate

Answer: A. Eminent Domain

Eminent Domain is the legal process that allows the government to take private property for public use, usually with compensation to the owner.

➡32. What is the term for a legal agreement that secures a loan with real property?

A. Deed of Trust

B. Bill of Sale

C. Lease

D. Promissory Note

Answer: A. Deed of Trust

A Deed of Trust is a legal agreement that secures a loan with real property and serves as protection for the lender.

➡33. What is the term for the legal right to use a portion of another person's property for a specific purpose, such as a driveway or pathway?

A. Easement

B. Lien

C. Covenant

D. Right of Way

Answer: A. Easement

An easement is the legal right to use a portion of another person's property for a specific purpose, such as a driveway or pathway.

➡34. What is the term for a legal document that transfers ownership of property from the seller to the buyer?

A. Warranty Deed

B. Bill of Sale

C. Title Certificate

D. Promissory Note

Answer: A. Warranty Deed

A Warranty Deed is a legal document that transfers ownership of property from the seller to the buyer.

➡ **35. What is the term for the legal right to pass through someone else's land?**

A. Right of Way

B. Easement

C. Zoning

D. Lien

Answer: A. Right of Way

Right of Way is the legal right to pass through someone else's land, often established through an easement.

➡ **36. What is the term for a legal document that outlines the terms of a rental agreement?**

A. Lease Agreement

B. Bill of Sale

C. Deed of Trust

D. Promissory Note

Answer: A. Lease Agreement

A Lease Agreement is a legal document that outlines the terms of a rental agreement between a landlord and tenant.

➡ **37. What is the term for the legal process of verifying the validity of a will?**

A. Probate

B. Eminent Domain

C. Foreclosure

D. Adverse Possession

Answer: A. Probate

Probate is the legal process of verifying the validity of a will and distributing the deceased's assets according to the will.

➡️**38. What is the term for a legal restriction placed on a property by a previous owner?**

A. Covenant

B. Easement

C. Lien

D. Zoning

Answer: A. Covenant

A covenant is a legal restriction placed on a property by a previous owner, often outlined in the deed.

➡️**39. What is the term for the legal process of dividing a large parcel of land into smaller lots?**

A. Subdivision

B. Zoning

C. Easement

D. Lien

Answer: A. Subdivision

Subdivision is the legal process of dividing a large parcel of land into smaller lots, often for the purpose of development.

➡40. What is the term for a legal document that grants someone the right to act on behalf of another in legal matters?

    A. Power of Attorney

    B. Lease Agreement

    C. Deed of Trust

    D. Promissory Note

Answer: A. Power of Attorney

Power of Attorney is a legal document that grants someone the right to act on behalf of another in legal matters.

➡41. What is the primary purpose of a deed restriction?

    A. To limit the use of the property

    B. To transfer ownership

    C. To secure a loan

    D. To establish easements

Answer: A. To limit the use of the property

Deed restrictions are used to limit the use of the property according to the terms set by the owner or the community.

➡42. What is the difference between a general warranty deed and a quitclaim deed?

    A. A general warranty deed provides no warranties

    B. A quitclaim deed provides full warranties

    C. A general warranty deed provides full warranties

    D. Both provide the same level of warranties

Answer: C. A general warranty deed provides full warranties

A general warranty deed provides the most protection to the buyer as it includes full warranties against any encumbrances.

➡️43. What is the role of a title company in a property transaction?

A. Financing the purchase

B. Ensuring the title is clear

C. Conducting home inspections

D. Setting the property's price

Answer: B. Ensuring the title is clear

The title company ensures that the title to a piece of real estate is legitimate and then issues title insurance for that property.

➡️44. What is the term for a written summary of a property's ownership history?

A. Title report

B. Chain of title

C. Deed of trust

D. Abstract of title

Answer: D. Abstract of title

An abstract of title is a written summary of a property's ownership history, which is used to determine the current status of the title.

➡️45. What is the purpose of a gift deed?

A. To transfer property as a gift

B. To secure a mortgage

C. To lease the property

D. To sell the property

Answer: A. To transfer property as a gift

A gift deed is used to transfer property ownership without any exchange of money.

➡ 46. What is a defeasible fee estate?

A. An estate that can be defeated or terminated

B. An estate that lasts forever

C. An estate that is free from encumbrances

D. An estate that is leased

Answer: A. An estate that can be defeated or terminated

A defeasible fee estate is a type of estate that can be defeated or terminated upon the occurrence of a specific event.

➡ 47. What is the primary purpose of a deed?

A. To prove ownership of personal property

B. To transfer ownership of real property

C. To outline the terms of a mortgage

D. To establish a rental agreement

Answer: B. To transfer ownership of real property

The primary purpose of a deed is to transfer ownership of real property from one party to another. It serves as a legal document that shows the change in ownership.

➡ 48. What is the primary purpose of a land contract?

A. To lease land

B. To sell land

C. To gift land

D. To mortgage land

Answer: B. To sell land

A land contract is primarily used to sell land, where the seller provides financing to the buyer.

→49. What is the term for the right of the government to take private property for public use?

A. Eminent domain

B. Escheat

C. Foreclosure

D. Adverse possession

Answer: A. Eminent domain

Eminent domain is the right of the government to take private property for public use, with compensation to the owner.

→50. What is the process of dividing a single property into smaller parcels?

A. Zoning

B. Subdivision

C. Partition

D. Condemnation

Answer: B. Subdivision

Subdivision is the process of dividing a single property into smaller parcels, often for the purpose of development.

Practice of Real Estate and Disclosures

The practice of real estate in Washington State is a regulated profession that requires strict adherence to laws, ethical standards, and best practices. One of the most critical aspects of real estate practice is the disclosure of relevant information. This chapter aims to provide a comprehensive guide on the practice of real estate and the importance of disclosures in Washington State.

Licensing and Continuing Education

Licensing Requirements

In Washington State, real estate agents must be licensed by the Washington State Department of Licensing (DOL). The requirements include completing a 90-hour pre-license education course, passing the state exam, and undergoing a background check.

Continuing Education

Licensed agents are required to complete 30 hours of continuing education every two years to renew their license. This ensures that agents are up-to-date with the latest laws and industry trends.

Role of a Real Estate Agent

Fiduciary Duties

Real estate agents have a fiduciary responsibility to their clients, which means they must act in their best interests. This includes confidentiality, full disclosure, obedience, loyalty, and accounting for all funds.

Buyer's Agent vs. Seller's Agent

A buyer's agent represents the buyer in a real estate transaction, while a seller's agent represents the seller. Dual agency, where an agent represents both parties, is legal in Washington but must be disclosed and consented to by all parties.

Disclosure Requirements

Seller Disclosure Statement

In Washington State, sellers are required to provide a Seller Disclosure Statement, which outlines the condition of the property. This includes information about the structure, systems, and any known defects or issues.

Material Facts

Agents are obligated to disclose material facts about a property. A material fact is any information that could affect a buyer's decision to purchase or a seller's willingness to sell.

Lead-Based Paint Disclosure

Federal law requires that sellers disclose any known presence of lead-based paint for homes built before 1978. Failure to do so can result in legal penalties.

Contracts and Agreements

Listing Agreement

A listing agreement is a contract between a seller and a real estate agent, outlining the terms under which the agent will market and sell the property.

Buyer Representation Agreement

This is a contract between a buyer and a real estate agent, specifying the services the agent will provide and the compensation they will receive.

Ethical Considerations

Code of Ethics

Real estate agents in Washington are expected to adhere to the National Association of Realtors (NAR) Code of Ethics, which sets the standard for professional conduct.

Conflict of Interest

Agents must disclose any conflict of interest, such as a personal relationship with a buyer or seller, and take steps to resolve it.

Technology and Real Estate Practice

Multiple Listing Service (MLS)

The MLS is a database where real estate agents list properties for sale. It's a crucial tool for market analysis and property valuation.

Virtual Tours and Online Marketing

With the advent of technology, virtual tours and online marketing have become essential tools for real estate agents.

Legal Consequences of Non-Disclosure

Failure to disclose material facts or misleading clients can result in legal action, including fines, license suspension, or even revocation.

Conclusion

The practice of real estate in Washington State is a complex field that requires a deep understanding of laws, ethics, and industry best practices. Disclosures play a crucial role in maintaining transparency and trust between all parties involved. By adhering to the state's stringent licensing requirements, continuing education, and ethical standards, real estate professionals can ensure a successful and lawful practice.

Mock Exam Practice of Real Estate and Disclosures

➡1. What is the primary focus of residential sales in real estate practice?

A. Lease agreements

B. Market trends

C. Zoning laws

D. Property management

Answer: B

Residential sales primarily focus on understanding market trends, property values, and the needs of clients.

➡2. What does a property manager NOT typically handle?

A. Rent collection

B. Maintenance and repairs

C. Property appraisals

D. Tenant relations

Answer: C

Property managers usually do not handle property appraisals; that's the job of a certified appraiser.

➡3. What is a material fact in real estate disclosures?

A. The color of the walls

B. The age of the roof

C. The seller's reason for moving

D. The brand of appliances in the home

Answer: B

Material facts include significant issues like the age of the roof, which could affect the property's value and condition.

➡4. What is the primary role of a leasing agent?

A. Property valuation
B. Finding tenants
C. Handling legal actions
D. Managing day-to-day operations

Answer: B

Leasing agents focus on finding tenants for vacant properties.

➡5. What must be disclosed about homes built before 1978?

A. Asbestos
B. Radon
C. Lead-based paint
D. All of the above

Answer: C

Federal law requires the disclosure of lead-based paint for homes built before 1978.

➡6. Who is responsible for providing a Seller's Property Disclosure?

A. Buyer
B. Seller
C. Real estate agent
D. Home inspector

Answer: B

The seller is responsible for filling out the Seller's Property Disclosure form.

➟7. What is NOT a type of disclosure in real estate?

A. Seller's Property Disclosure

B. Agency Disclosures

C. Financial Disclosures

D. Buyer's Property Disclosure

Answer: D

There is no such thing as a Buyer's Property Disclosure; the seller provides all necessary disclosures.

➟8. What does a real estate appraiser provide?

A. Legal advice

B. Estimated property value

C. Lease agreements

D. Tenant screening

Answer: B

Real estate appraisers provide an estimated value of a property.

➟9. What is included in natural hazards disclosures?

A. Property age

B. Utility availability

C. Flood risk

D. Previous owners

Answer: C

Natural hazards disclosures may include information on flood risk, earthquakes, and other natural disasters.

➡ 10. What is the primary ethical obligation of a real estate professional?

A. Maximizing profit

B. Acting in the best interests of their clients

C. Avoiding legal repercussions

D. Networking

Answer: B

Real estate professionals are ethically bound to act in the best interests of their clients.

➡ 11. What is the primary purpose of a Comparative Market Analysis (CMA)?

A. To determine property taxes

B. To set a listing price

C. To assess zoning laws

D. To evaluate mortgage options

Answer: B

A Comparative Market Analysis is primarily used to set a listing price for a property based on similar properties in the area.

➡ 12. What does the acronym RESPA stand for?

A. Real Estate Settlement Procedures Act

B. Residential Estate Sales Professional Association

C. Real Estate Service Providers Act

D. Residential Environmental Safety Protocol Act

Answer: A

RESPA stands for Real Estate Settlement Procedures Act, which regulates closing costs and settlement procedures.

➡️13. What is the role of a fiduciary in real estate?

A. To provide financing

B. To act in the best interest of the client

C. To appraise the property

D. To market the property

Answer: B

A fiduciary is obligated to act in the best interest of the client.

➡️14. What is NOT a common type of real estate fraud?

A. Property flipping

B. Equity skimming

C. False advertising

D. Open listing

Answer: D

Open listing is a type of listing agreement, not a form of real estate fraud.

➡️15. What is the main purpose of a title search?

A. To find the property's market value

B. To verify the legal owner of the property

C. To assess the property's condition

D. To determine the property's zoning status

Answer: B

The main purpose of a title search is to verify the legal owner of the property.

→16. What is a latent defect?

    A. A defect that is visible during a walk-through

    B. A defect that is hidden and not easily discoverable

    C. A defect that has been repaired

    D. A defect listed in the property disclosure

Answer: B

A latent defect is a hidden defect that is not easily discoverable during a routine inspection.

→17. What is the primary purpose of a home inspection?

    A. To assess the property's market value

    B. To identify any defects or issues with the property

    C. To verify the property's legal status

    D. To finalize the mortgage terms

Answer: B

The primary purpose of a home inspection is to identify any defects or issues with the property.

→18. What is a short sale?

    A. A quick sale process

    B. Selling the property for less than the mortgage owed

    C. A sale with few contingencies

    D. A sale where the buyer pays in cash

Answer: B

A short sale is when the property is sold for less than the amount owed on the mortgage.

➡19. What is earnest money?

A. The commission for the real estate agent

B. A deposit made by the buyer

C. The final payment at closing

D. Money paid for a home inspection

Answer: B

Earnest money is a deposit made by the buyer to show their serious intent to purchase the property.

➡20. What does a contingency in a real estate contract allow?

A. Immediate possession of the property

B. The buyer to back out under specific conditions

C. The seller to change the listing price

D. The real estate agent to collect a higher commission

Answer: B

A contingency allows the buyer to back out of the purchase under specific conditions without losing their earnest money.

➡21. What is the primary role of the Multiple Listing Service (MLS)?

A. To provide mortgage rates

B. To list properties for sale

C. To regulate real estate agents

D. To assess property taxes

Answer: B

The primary role of the MLS is to list properties for sale, making it easier for agents to find properties for their clients.

→22. What is a dual agency?

A. When two agents represent the buyer

B. When one agent represents both the buyer and the seller

C. When two agents represent the seller

D. When an agent represents two buyers in the same transaction

Answer: B

Dual agency occurs when one agent represents both the buyer and the seller in a real estate transaction.

→23. What is the main purpose of a seller's disclosure?

A. To list the price of the property

B. To disclose any known defects or issues with the property

C. To describe the property's features

D. To outline the commission rates

Answer: B

The main purpose of a seller's disclosure is to disclose any known defects or issues with the property.

→24. What does the term "underwater mortgage" mean?

A. A mortgage with a high interest rate

B. A mortgage that is higher than the property's value

C. A mortgage for a property near a body of water

D. A mortgage that has been paid off

Answer: B

An underwater mortgage is when the remaining mortgage balance is higher than the current market value of the property.

25. What is a "pocket listing"?

A. A listing that is not yet on the market

B. A listing that is only shared with a select group of agents

C. A listing that has been sold

D. A listing that is under contract

Answer: B

A pocket listing is a listing that is not publicly advertised and is only shared with a select group of agents.

26. What is the main purpose of a buyer's agent?

A. To list properties for sale

B. To represent the buyer's interests

C. To conduct home inspections

D. To provide financing options

Answer: B

The main purpose of a buyer's agent is to represent the interests of the buyer in a real estate transaction.

27. What is a "balloon payment"?

A. A small monthly payment

B. A large final payment at the end of a mortgage term

C. A payment made halfway through the mortgage term

D. A payment made to the real estate agent

Answer: B

A balloon payment is a large final payment due at the end of a mortgage term.

28. What is "redlining"?

A. Drawing property boundaries

B. Discriminatory practice in lending or insurance

C. Highlighting important clauses in a contract

D. Marking properties that are under contract

Answer: B

Redlining is a discriminatory practice where services like lending or insurance are denied or priced higher for residents of certain areas.

29. What is the main purpose of an escrow account?

A. To hold the earnest money deposit

B. To pay the real estate agent's commission

C. To store the property's title

D. To hold funds for property taxes and insurance

Answer: D

The main purpose of an escrow account is to hold funds for property taxes and insurance.

30. What is a "contingent offer"?

A. An offer that is higher than the listing price

B. An offer that is dependent on certain conditions being met

C. An offer that has been accepted but not yet closed

D. An offer that is non-negotiable

Answer: B

A contingent offer is an offer that is dependent on certain conditions being met, such as financing or a satisfactory home inspection.

→31. What is the primary role of a "listing agent"?

A. To represent the buyer in a transaction

B. To represent the seller in a transaction

C. To conduct the home inspection

D. To provide financing options

Answer: B

The primary role of a listing agent is to represent the seller in a real estate transaction, helping them to sell their property.

→32. What is a "short sale"?

A. A quick sale of a property

B. Selling a property for less than the mortgage owed

C. Selling a property without an agent

D. A discounted sale for a quick closing

Answer: B

A short sale is when a property is sold for less than the amount owed on the mortgage.

→33. What is "title insurance"?

A. Insurance for property damage

B. Insurance that protects against defects in the title

C. Insurance for the mortgage lender

D. Insurance for the real estate agent

Answer: B

Title insurance protects against defects in the title to the property.

→34. What is "earnest money"?

A. Money paid to the real estate agent

B. Money paid to secure a contract

C. Money paid for a home inspection

D. Money paid for closing costs

Answer: B

Earnest money is a deposit made to a seller to show the buyer's good faith in a transaction.

➡35. **What is a "FSBO" listing?**

A. For Sale By Owner

B. For Sale By Operator

C. For Sale Before Offer

D. For Sale By Order

Answer: A

FSBO stands for "For Sale By Owner," indicating that the property is being sold without a real estate agent.

➡36. **What is "amortization"?**

A. The process of increasing property value

B. The process of paying off a loan over time

C. The process of transferring property

D. The process of evaluating a property's worth

Answer: B

Amortization is the process of paying off a loan over time through regular payments.

➡37. **What is a "home warranty"?**

A. A guarantee on the home's structure

B. A guarantee on the home's appliances and systems

C. A guarantee on the home's value

D. A guarantee on the home's location

Answer: B

A home warranty is a service contract that covers the repair or replacement of important home system components and appliances.

→38. What is "zoning"?

A. The process of measuring a property

B. The division of land into areas for specific uses

C. The process of evaluating a property's value

D. The process of transferring property

Answer: B

Zoning is the division of land into areas designated for specific uses, such as residential, commercial, or industrial.

→39. What is a "pre-approval letter"?

A. A letter confirming the property's value

B. A letter confirming mortgage eligibility

C. A letter confirming the property's condition

D. A letter confirming the real estate agent's credentials

Answer: B

A pre-approval letter is a letter from a lender indicating that a buyer is eligible for a mortgage up to a certain amount.

→40. What is "escrow"?

A. A type of mortgage

B. A legal arrangement where a third party holds assets

C. A type of home inspection

D. A type of real estate contract

Answer: B

Escrow is a legal arrangement in which a third party holds assets on behalf of the buyer and seller.

→ 41. What is the purpose of a "Seller's Disclosure Statement"?

A. To disclose the seller's financial status

B. To disclose any known defects or issues with the property

C. To disclose the commission rate of the real estate agents

D. To disclose the buyer's financing options

Answer: B

The Seller's Disclosure Statement is used to disclose any known defects or issues with the property to potential buyers.

→ 42. What does "dual agency" mean in real estate?

A. Two agents working for the same brokerage

B. An agent representing both the buyer and the seller

C. Two buyers competing for the same property

D. Two lenders involved in the financing

Answer: B

Dual agency occurs when a real estate agent represents both the buyer and the seller in the same transaction.

➠43. What is the primary purpose of a "title search"?

A. To find the property's market value

B. To check for any liens or encumbrances on the property

C. To assess the property's condition

D. To determine the zoning laws affecting the property

Answer: B

The primary purpose of a title search is to check for any liens or encumbrances on the property.

➠44. What does "FSBO" stand for?

A. For Sale By Owner

B. Full Service Brokerage Option

C. Fixed Selling Bonus Offer

D. Final Sale Before Offer

Answer: A

FSBO stands for "For Sale By Owner," indicating that the property is being sold directly by the owner without the representation of a real estate agent.

➠45. What is a "contingency" in a real estate contract?

A. A mandatory clause

B. A binding agreement

C. A condition that must be met for the contract to proceed

D. A non-negotiable term

Answer: C

A contingency is a condition that must be met for the contract to proceed.

→46. **What is the role of an "escrow agent"?**

A. To market the property

B. To hold and disburse funds during a transaction

C. To negotiate the contract terms

D. To inspect the property

Answer: B

The role of an escrow agent is to hold and disburse funds during a real estate transaction.

→47. **What does "amortization" refer to?**

A. The process of increasing property value

B. The process of paying off a loan over time

C. The process of transferring property ownership

D. The process of evaluating a property's worth

Answer: B

Amortization refers to the process of paying off a loan over time through regular payments.

→48. **What is the "right of first refusal" in a real estate context?**

A. The right to refuse a home inspection

B. The right to be the first to make an offer on a property

C. The right to refuse to pay closing costs

D. The right to refuse to honor a contract

Answer: B

The right of first refusal gives a person the opportunity to be the first to make an offer on a property before the owner sells it to someone else.

➠49. What does "encumbrance" refer to in real estate?

A. A type of insurance policy

B. A claim or lien on a property

C. A type of mortgage loan

D. A legal restriction on property use

Answer: B

An encumbrance is a claim or lien on a property that affects its use or transfer.

➠50. What does "under contract" mean in real estate?

A. The property is being appraised

B. The property is available for sale

C. The property has an accepted offer but has not yet closed

D. The property is off the market

Answer: C

"Under contract" means that the property has an accepted offer but the sale has not yet closed.

Contracts

Contracts are the backbone of any real estate transaction. They provide the legal framework that governs the relationship between buyers, sellers, and real estate professionals. In Washington State, there are several types of contracts that you'll encounter in the real estate industry, each with its own set of rules, obligations, and legal implications. This chapter will delve into the intricacies of these contracts, offering a comprehensive guide for both real estate professionals and consumers.

Types of Real Estate Contracts

Listing Agreement

A listing agreement is a contract between a seller and a real estate broker or agent. It outlines the terms under which the broker will market and sell the property. There are different types of listing agreements, such as exclusive right to sell, exclusive agency, and open listing, each with its own set of terms and conditions.

Purchase and Sale Agreement

This is the primary contract in any real estate transaction. It outlines the terms and conditions under which a property will be sold, including the price, closing date, and any contingencies.

Buyer Representation Agreement

This contract outlines the relationship between the buyer and the real estate agent. It specifies the services the agent will provide and the commission they will receive.

Lease Agreement

In rental transactions, the lease agreement outlines the terms under which a tenant will rent a property from a landlord.

Essential Elements of a Contract

Offer and Acceptance

For a contract to be valid, there must be a clear offer from one party and an unequivocal acceptance from the other.

Consideration

This refers to something of value that is exchanged between the parties. In real estate, this is often the property itself and the money paid for it.

Legal Capacity

Both parties must have the legal capacity to enter into a contract, meaning they must be of legal age and sound mind.

Legality of Purpose

The contract must be for a legal purpose. Contracts for illegal activities are not enforceable.

Contingencies in Real Estate Contracts

Financing Contingency

This allows the buyer to back out if they are unable to secure financing by a certain date.

Inspection Contingency

This gives the buyer the right to have the property inspected and to request repairs or back out of the deal based on the findings.

Appraisal Contingency

This protects the buyer if the property is appraised for less than the purchase price.

Contract Termination

Mutual Agreement

Both parties can agree to terminate the contract.

Breach of Contract

If one party fails to fulfill their obligations, the other may have the right to terminate the contract.

Expiration

Some contracts have a set term and will expire if not executed within that timeframe.

Legal Remedies for Breach of Contract

Specific Performance

The court may order the breaching party to fulfill their obligations under the contract.

Damages

The injured party may be entitled to monetary compensation.

Rescission

The contract is canceled, and both parties are returned to their original positions.

Electronic Contracts and E-Signatures

Washington State recognizes electronic contracts and e-signatures as legally binding, provided they meet certain criteria under the federal E-SIGN Act and the Washington Electronic Authentication Act.

Ethical Considerations

Real estate professionals must adhere to a high standard of ethics when dealing with contracts. This includes full disclosure, honesty, and acting in the best interest of the client.

Conclusion

Contracts are a complex but essential part of real estate transactions in Washington State. Understanding the different types of contracts and their legal implications is crucial for anyone involved in the real estate industry. From listing agreements to purchase and sale contracts, each serves a specific purpose and requires careful consideration and understanding. Failure to adhere to the terms of these contracts can result in legal consequences, making it imperative to consult with professionals and legal advisors when entering into any real estate contract.

Mock Exam Contracts

➡1. What is the primary purpose of a Purchase Agreement in real estate?

A. To outline the commission for the real estate agent

B. To set the stage for the relationship between buyer and seller

C. To provide a warranty for the property

D. To list the property on MLS

Answer: B

The Purchase Agreement serves as the cornerstone of any real estate transaction, outlining the terms and conditions between the buyer and seller.

➡2. Which type of lease requires the tenant to pay a flat rent while the landlord pays for all property charges?

A. Gross Lease

B. Net Lease

C. Triple Net Lease

D. Modified Gross Lease

Answer: A

In a Gross Lease, the tenant pays a flat rent and the landlord is responsible for all property charges.

➡3. What is "Consideration" in a contract?

A. A thoughtful gesture

B. Money or something of value exchanged

C. A legal requirement

D. A counteroffer

Answer: B

Consideration refers to something of value that is exchanged between parties in a contract. It can be money, services, or even a promise.

➡️**4. What happens in a Material Breach of contract?**

A. A minor failure in performance

B. A significant failure in performance

C. A legal dispute

D. Contract is automatically renewed

Answer: B

A Material Breach is a significant failure in performance that allows the other party to seek remedies.

➡️**5. Which clause in a contract specifies what will happen if issues are found during an inspection?**

A. Contingency Clause

B. Disclosure Clause

C. Inspection Clause

D. Arbitration Clause

Answer: C

The Inspection Clause outlines the type of inspection, who will conduct it, and what actions will be taken if issues are found.

➡️**6. What does a "Straight Option" in an Option Agreement provide?**

A. The right to lease the property

B. The exclusive right to purchase within a certain time

C. The right to sublease the property

D. The right to first refusal

Answer: B

A Straight Option gives the buyer the exclusive right to purchase the property within a specified time frame.

➡7. Who cannot legally enter into a contract?

A. A licensed real estate agent

B. A minor

C. A property manager

D. A real estate investor

Answer: B

Minors are not legally competent to enter into contracts.

➡8. What is the primary purpose of Disclosure Clauses?

A. To outline the commission structure

B. To state federal and state requirements for property disclosure

C. To specify the type of inspection

D. To set the rent amount in a lease

Answer: B

Disclosure Clauses are used to state federal and state requirements for property disclosure, such as the presence of lead paint.

➡9. What is a Conditional Sale Agreement?

A. The property is sold as-is

B. The sale is conditional upon certain criteria

C. The buyer has the option to purchase later

D. The seller can back out at any time

Answer: B

A Conditional Sale Agreement means the sale is conditional upon certain criteria being met, such as the sale of the buyer's current home.

➡10. What is the legal status of a contract for illegal activities?

A. Valid

B. Null and void

C. Conditional

D. Binding

Answer: B

Contracts for illegal activities are considered null and void.

➡11. What is the role of an "Escrow Agent" in a real estate contract?

A. To market the property

B. To hold and disburse funds

C. To conduct inspections

D. To negotiate terms

Answer: B

The Escrow Agent holds and disburses funds according to the terms of the contract.

➡12. Which of the following is NOT a required element for a contract to be valid?

A. Offer and acceptance

B. Consideration

C. Legal purpose

D. Notarization

Answer: D

Notarization is not a required element for a contract to be valid.

➡13. What is the "Statute of Frauds" in relation to contracts?

A. A law that makes oral contracts illegal

B. A law that requires certain contracts to be in writing

C. A law that prevents fraudulent activities

D. A law that nullifies all previous contracts

Answer: B

The Statute of Frauds requires certain contracts, like those for real estate, to be in writing to be enforceable.

➡14. What does "Time is of the Essence" mean in a contract?

A. The contract has no expiration date

B. The contract must be executed within a specific timeframe

C. The contract can be modified at any time

D. The contract is not urgent

Answer: B

"Time is of the Essence" means that the contract must be executed within a specific timeframe, and delays could lead to penalties or termination of the contract.

➡15. What is a "Right of First Refusal"?

A. The right to reject any offer

B. The right to match or better any offer received by the seller

C. The right to be the first to view a property

D. The right to terminate a contract without penalty

Answer: B

The Right of First Refusal allows the holder to match or better any offer received by the seller before the property is sold to another party.

→16. What is a "Contingent Contract"?

A. A contract that is dependent on certain conditions being met

B. A contract that is legally binding

C. A contract that has been terminated

D. A contract that is in the negotiation phase

Answer: A

A Contingent Contract is dependent on certain conditions being met, such as financing approval or a satisfactory home inspection.

→17. What is "Specific Performance"?

A. A clause that specifies the responsibilities of each party

B. A legal remedy for breach of contract

C. A type of contract used in commercial real estate

D. A measure of a real estate agent's effectiveness

Answer: B

Specific Performance is a legal remedy that forces the breaching party to fulfill the terms of the contract.

→18. What is the purpose of a "Hold Harmless Clause"?

A. To protect the buyer from market fluctuations

B. To protect one or both parties from liability for the actions of the other

C. To hold the property off the market for a specific period

D. To hold the buyer's deposit in escrow

Answer: B

A Hold Harmless Clause protects one or both parties from liability for the actions or negligence of the other party.

➡19. What is a "Bilateral Contract"?

A. A contract where only one party is obligated to perform

B. A contract where both parties are obligated to perform

C. A contract that is null and void

D. A contract that has been terminated

Answer: B

In a Bilateral Contract, both parties are obligated to perform their respective duties.

➡20. What is the "Implied Covenant of Good Faith and Fair Dealing"?

A. A written clause in every contract

B. An unwritten obligation for parties to act honestly and not cheat each other

C. A legal doctrine that makes all contracts public

D. A requirement for all contracts to be reviewed by a lawyer

Answer: B

The Implied Covenant of Good Faith and Fair Dealing is an unwritten obligation that requires parties to act honestly and not cheat or mislead each other.

➡21. What is a "Unilateral Contract"?

A. A contract where only one party is obligated to perform

B. A contract where both parties are obligated to perform

C. A contract that is null and void

D. A contract that has been terminated

Answer: A

In a Unilateral Contract, only one party is obligated to perform, while the other has the option but not the obligation to perform.

→22. What is "Liquidated Damages"?

A. The actual damages suffered due to a breach

B. A pre-determined amount to be paid in case of a breach

C. The refundable part of a deposit

D. The non-refundable part of a deposit

Answer: B

Liquidated Damages are a pre-determined amount agreed upon by the parties to be paid in case of a breach of contract.

→23. What is "Novation"?

A. The act of renewing a contract

B. The act of replacing one party in a contract with another

C. The act of nullifying a contract

D. The act of negotiating the terms of a contract

Answer: B

Novation is the act of replacing one party in a contract with another, effectively transferring the obligations to the new party.

→24. What is an "Addendum"?

A. A change to the original contract

B. A separate agreement that is included with the original contract

C. A summary of the contract

D. A legal interpretation of the contract

Answer: B

An Addendum is a separate agreement that is included with the original contract to add or clarify terms.

→25. **What is "Recission"?**

A. The act of renewing a contract

B. The act of terminating a contract and restoring parties to their original positions

C. The act of transferring a contract

D. The act of amending a contract

Answer: B

Recission is the act of terminating a contract and restoring the parties to their original positions, as if the contract had never existed.

→26. **What is "Parol Evidence"?**

A. Written evidence

B. Oral evidence

C. Photographic evidence

D. Video evidence

Answer: B

Parol Evidence refers to oral statements or agreements that are not included in the written contract.

→27. **What is a "Counteroffer"?**

A. An acceptance of the original offer

B. A rejection of the original offer

C. A new offer made in response to an original offer

D. A legal requirement for all contracts

Answer: C

A Counteroffer is a new offer made in response to an original offer, effectively rejecting the original offer.

➡28. **What is "Earnest Money"?**

A. Money paid to confirm a contract

B. Money paid to a real estate agent

C. Money held in escrow

D. Money paid for a home inspection

Answer: A

Earnest Money is money paid to confirm a contract, showing the buyer's serious intent to purchase.

➡29. **What is "Force Majeure"?**

A. A clause that frees both parties from liability in case of an extraordinary event

B. A clause that holds both parties liable regardless of circumstances

C. A clause that allows for price negotiation

D. A clause that requires a third-party mediator

Answer: A

Force Majeure is a clause that frees both parties from liability in case of an extraordinary event, like a natural disaster, that prevents one or both parties from fulfilling the contract.

➡30. **What is "Severability"?**

A. The ability to separate a contract into individual clauses

B. The ability to terminate a contract without penalty

C. The ability to transfer a contract to another party

D. The ability to amend a contract after signing

Answer: A

Severability is the ability to separate a contract into individual clauses, so that if one clause is found to be unenforceable, the rest of the contract remains in effect.

➡ **31. What does "Statute of Frauds" require for a real estate contract to be enforceable?**

A. Verbal agreement

B. Written and signed agreement

C. Notarized agreement

D. Witnessed agreement

Answer: B

The Statute of Frauds requires that a real estate contract must be in writing and signed by the parties to be enforceable.

➡ **32. What is "Specific Performance"?**

A. Monetary compensation for breach of contract

B. Forcing a party to carry out the terms of the contract

C. Nullifying the contract

D. Amending the contract

Answer: B

Specific Performance is a legal remedy that forces a party to carry out the terms of the contract as agreed.

➡ **33. What is "Time is of the Essence" in a contract?**

A. A clause that allows for flexible deadlines

B. A clause that makes deadlines strictly binding

C. A clause that nullifies the contract after a certain time

D. A clause that allows for automatic renewal of the contract

Answer: B

"Time is of the Essence" is a clause that makes deadlines strictly binding, and failure to meet them could lead to breach of contract.

➡ **34. What is an "Open Listing"?**

A. A listing agreement with multiple brokers

B. A listing agreement with one broker

C. A listing that is not publicly advertised

D. A listing that is only advertised within a brokerage

Answer: A

An Open Listing is a listing agreement where the seller can employ multiple brokers who can bring buyers to the property.

➡ **35. What is a "Net Listing"?**

A. A listing where the broker's commission is a percentage of the sale price

B. A listing where the broker keeps all amounts above a certain price

C. A listing where the broker charges a flat fee

D. A listing where the broker's commission is paid by the buyer

Answer: B

In a Net Listing, the broker agrees to sell the owner's property for a set price, and anything above that price is kept as the broker's commission.

➡ **36. What is a "Contingency" in a contract?**

A. A fixed term

B. A condition that must be met for the contract to be binding

C. A penalty for breach of contract

D. An optional term

Answer: B

A Contingency is a condition that must be met for the contract to proceed to closing.

➡37. What is "Due Diligence" in the context of a real estate contract?

A. The buyer's investigation of the property

B. The seller's disclosure of property defects

C. The broker's marketing efforts

D. The lender's appraisal of the property

Answer: A

Due Diligence refers to the buyer's investigation of the property to discover any issues that were not disclosed.

➡38. What is "Escrow"?

A. A legal process to resolve disputes

B. A third-party account where funds are held until conditions are met

C. A type of mortgage

D. A tax levied on property sales

Answer: B

Escrow is a third-party account where funds or assets are held until contractual conditions are met.

➡39. What is "Right of First Refusal"?

A. The right to be the first to purchase a property

B. The right to refuse any offer on a property

C. The right to terminate a contract

D. The right to amend a contract

Answer: A

Right of First Refusal gives a person the opportunity to be the first to purchase a property before the owner sells it to someone else.

➡40. What is "Joint Tenancy"?

A. Ownership by one individual

B. Ownership by two or more individuals with equal shares

C. Ownership by a corporation

D. Ownership by tenants

Answer: B

Joint Tenancy is a form of ownership where two or more individuals own property with equal shares and have the right of survivorship.

➡41. What is the primary purpose of a "Letter of Intent" in a real estate transaction?

A. To serve as a binding contract

B. To outline the terms under which a contract will be negotiated

C. To legally transfer property

D. To terminate an existing contract

Answer: B

A Letter of Intent serves to outline the terms under which the parties will negotiate a contract. It is generally not binding.

➡42. What does "Time is of the Essence" mean in a real estate contract?

A. The contract has an indefinite period

B. The contract must be executed within a specific timeframe

C. The contract can be terminated at any time

D. The contract is not time-sensitive

Answer: B

"Time is of the Essence" means that the contract must be executed within a specific timeframe, and failure to do so could result in penalties or termination of the contract.

➡43. What is the purpose of an "Addendum" in a real estate contract?

A. To correct a typo or error

B. To add additional terms or conditions

C. To terminate the contract

D. To renew the contract

Answer: B

An Addendum is used to add additional terms or conditions to an existing contract, effectively modifying it.

➡44. What is the effect of a "Waiver" in a contract?

A. It adds a new term to the contract

B. It removes a party's right to enforce a term of the contract

C. It extends the contract's duration

D. It makes the contract voidable

Answer: B

A waiver removes a party's right to enforce a particular term of the contract, essentially giving up that right.

➠45. What is "Specific Performance" in the context of a real estate contract?

A. Monetary compensation

B. Carrying out the exact terms of the contract

C. Termination of the contract

D. An optional performance

Answer: B

Specific Performance refers to carrying out the exact terms of the contract, usually enforced through a court order.

➠46. What does "Novation" mean in a contract?

A. Renewal of the contract

B. Replacement of one party with another

C. Addition of a new term

D. Termination of the contract

Answer: B

Novation means the replacement of one party in the contract with another, effectively transferring the obligations to the new party.

➠47. What does "Force Majeure" refer to in a contract?

A. A type of fraud

B. An act of God or unforeseen circumstances

C. A breach of contract

D. A type of contingency

Answer: B

Force Majeure refers to unforeseen circumstances or "acts of God" that prevent one or both parties from fulfilling the contract. It usually allows for the contract to be terminated or suspended.

➡48. What is the role of an "Escrow Agent"?

A. To negotiate the contract
B. To hold and disburse funds or documents
C. To enforce the contract
D. To terminate the contract

Answer: B

An Escrow Agent holds and disburses funds or documents as per the terms of the contract.

➡49. What is "Right of First Refusal" in a real estate contract?

A. The right to back out of the contract first
B. The right to match any offer received by the seller
C. The right to inspect the property first
D. The right to make the first offer on a property

Answer: B

Right of First Refusal gives a party the right to match any offer received by the seller, usually before the property is sold to another buyer.

➡50. What is "Earnest Money" in the context of a real estate contract?

A. The commission for the real estate agent
B. A deposit made by the buyer to show good faith
C. The final payment made at closing
D. A refundable deposit

Answer: B

Earnest Money is a deposit made by the buyer to show good faith and secure the contract.

It is usually non-refundable and is applied to the purchase price.

Real Estate Calculations

Real estate calculations are an integral part of the real estate industry. Whether you're an agent, a buyer, or an investor, understanding the numbers is crucial. This chapter will delve into the most important calculations you'll encounter, from mortgage payments to investment returns.

Property Valuation

Comparative Market Analysis (CMA)

A Comparative Market Analysis (CMA) is the cornerstone of property valuation. It involves comparing the property in question to similar properties ("comparables" or "comps") that have recently sold in the area.

Formula:

Property Value = Average Price of Comparable Properties x (1 + Adjustment Factor)}

Why It Matters:
Understanding how to accurately perform a CMA can mean the difference between overpricing a property, causing it to sit on the market, or underpricing it and losing money.

Capitalization Rate

The capitalization rate, or cap rate, is another essential metric for property valuation, particularly for income-generating properties.

Formula:

$$\text{Cap Rate} = \frac{Net\ Operating\ Income}{Current\ Market\ Value}$$

Why It Matters:

The cap rate gives you a quick way to compare the profitability of different investment properties.

Financing Calculations

Mortgage Payments

Mortgage calculations are essential for both buyers and real estate professionals to understand.

Formula:

$$M = P \times \frac{r(1+r)^n}{(1+r)^n - 1}$$

Where :

M is the monthly payment,

P is the principal loan amount,

r is the monthly interest rate, and

n is the number of payments.

Why It Matters:

Knowing how to calculate mortgage payments allows you to assess the affordability of a property and helps in planning long-term finances.

Loan-to-Value Ratio (LTV)

The Loan-to-Value ratio is a risk assessment metric that lenders use.

Formula:

$$LTV = \frac{Loan\ Amount}{Appraised\ Value} \times 100$$

Why It Matters:

A high LTV ratio might mean a riskier loan from a lender's perspective, potentially requiring the borrower to purchase mortgage insurance.

Investment Calculations

Return on Investment (ROI)

ROI is a measure of the profitability of an investment.

Formula:

$$\text{ROI} = \frac{Net\ Profit}{Cost\ of\ Investment} \times 100$$

Why It Matters:

ROI gives you a snapshot of the investment's performance, helping you compare it against other investment opportunities.

Cash-on-Cash Return

This metric gives you the annual return on your investment based on the cash flow and the amount of money you've invested.

Formula:

$$\text{Cash-on-Cash Return} = \frac{Annual\ Cash\ Flow}{Total\ Cash\ Invested} \times 100$$

Why It Matters:

Cash-on-cash return is crucial for understanding the cash income you're generating compared to the cash invested, providing a more accurate picture of an investment's performance.

Area and Volume Calculations

Square Footage

Square footage is the measure of an area, and it's one of the most basic calculations in real estate.

Formula:

Area = Length x Width

Why It Matters:

Square footage affects everything from listing prices to renovation costs, so getting it right is crucial.

Cubic Footage

Cubic footage is often used in commercial real estate to determine the volume of a space.

Formula:

Volume = Length x Width x Height

Why It Matters:

In commercial settings, cubic footage can be essential for understanding how a space can be used.

Prorations and Commissions

Prorations

Prorations are used to divide property taxes, insurance premiums, or other costs between the buyer and seller.

Formula:

$$\textbf{Proration Amount} = \frac{Annual\ Cost}{365} \times \textbf{Number of Days}$$

Why It Matters:
Prorations ensure that both parties are only paying for their share of the costs during the time they own the property.

Commission Calculation

Commissions are the lifeblood of most real estate agents and brokers.

Formula:

Commission = Sale Price x Commission Rate

Why It Matters:
Understanding how commissions are calculated can help agents set realistic business goals and expectations.

Conclusion

Mastering these calculations is not just a requirement for passing various real estate exams; it's a necessity for a successful career in real estate. This chapter has covered the essential calculations any real estate professional needs to understand.

Mock Exam Real Estate Calculations

➡1. What is the formula for calculating the Loan-to-Value ratio?

   A. Loan Amount / Appraised Value

   B. Appraised Value / Loan Amount

   C. Loan Amount × Appraised Value

   D. Appraised Value × Loan Amount

Answer: A

The Loan-to-Value ratio is calculated as Loan Amount divided by Appraised Value.

➡2. What does ROI stand for?

   A. Return On Investment

   B. Rate Of Interest

   C. Real Estate Opportunity

   D. Rate Of Inflation

Answer: A

ROI stands for Return On Investment, which measures the profitability of an investment.

➡3. What is the formula for calculating square footage?

   A. Length × Width

   B. Length × Height

   C. Length + Width

   D. Length / Width

Answer: A

Square footage is calculated by multiplying the length by the width of the area.

➡️4. What is the formula for calculating mortgage payments?

A. $P \times (r(1+r)^n) / ((1+r)^n-1)$

B. $P \times r \times n$

C. $P / r \times n$

D. $P \times n / r$

Answer: A

The formula for calculating mortgage payments is $P \times (r(1+r)^n) / ((1+r)^n-1)$.

➡️5. What is the formula for calculating the capitalization rate?

A. Net Operating Income / Current Market Value

B. Current Market Value / Net Operating Income

C. Net Operating Income $\times$ Current Market Value

D. Current Market Value $\times$ Net Operating Income

Answer: A

The capitalization rate is calculated as Net Operating Income divided by Current Market Value.

➡️6. What does CMA stand for in real estate calculations?

A. Comparative Market Analysis

B. Capital Market Assessment

C. Current Market Appraisal

D. Comparative Monetary Assessment

Answer: A

CMA stands for Comparative Market Analysis, used for property valuation.

➡7. What is the formula for calculating Cash-on-Cash Return?

   A. Annual Cash Flow / Total Cash Invested × 100

   B. Total Cash Invested / Annual Cash Flow × 100

   C. Annual Cash Flow × Total Cash Invested

   D. Total Cash Invested × Annual Cash Flow

Answer: A

Cash-on-Cash Return is calculated as Annual Cash Flow divided by Total Cash Invested, multiplied by 100.

➡8. What is the formula for calculating prorations?

   A. Annual Cost / 365 × Number of Days

   B. Annual Cost × 365 / Number of Days

   C. Number of Days / Annual Cost × 365

   D. Number of Days × Annual Cost / 365

Answer: A

Prorations are calculated as Annual Cost divided by 365, multiplied by the Number of Days.

➡9. What is the formula for calculating cubic footage?

   A. Length × Width × Height

   B. Length × Width

   C. Length × Height

   D. Width × Height

Answer: A

Cubic footage is calculated by multiplying the length, width, and height of the space.

➡10. What is the formula for calculating commissions?

A. Sale Price × Commission Rate

B. Commission Rate × Sale Price

C. Sale Price / Commission Rate

D. Commission Rate / Sale Price

Answer: A

Commissions are calculated as Sale Price multiplied by Commission Rate.

➡11. What is the formula for calculating Gross Rent Multiplier (GRM)?

A. Property Price / Gross Annual Rents

B. Gross Annual Rents / Property Price

C. Property Price × Gross Annual Rents

D. Gross Annual Rents × Property Price

Answer: A

The Gross Rent Multiplier (GRM) is calculated by dividing the property price by the gross annual rents.

➡12. What is the formula for calculating depreciation?

A. (Cost of the Property - Salvage Value) / Useful Life

B. (Salvage Value - Cost of the Property) / Useful Life

C. Cost of the Property × Salvage Value

D. Salvage Value × Cost of the Property

Answer: A

Depreciation is calculated by subtracting the salvage value from the cost of the property and dividing by its useful life.

➡13. What does PITI stand for in mortgage calculations?

A. Principal, Interest, Taxes, Insurance

B. Payment, Interest, Taxes, Insurance

C. Principal, Income, Taxes, Insurance

D. Payment, Income, Taxes, Insurance

Answer: A

PITI stands for Principal, Interest, Taxes, and Insurance, which are the four components of a mortgage payment.

➡14. What is the formula for calculating equity?

A. Market Value - Mortgage Balance

B. Mortgage Balance - Market Value

C. Market Value × Mortgage Balance

D. Mortgage Balance × Market Value

Answer: A

Equity is calculated as the market value of the property minus the mortgage balance.

➡15. What is the formula for calculating net operating income (NOI)?

A. Gross Income - Operating Expenses

B. Operating Expenses - Gross Income

C. Gross Income × Operating Expenses

D. Operating Expenses × Gross Income

Answer: A

Net Operating Income (NOI) is calculated by subtracting operating expenses from gross income.

➡16. What is the formula for calculating the break-even point?

A. Fixed Costs / (Selling Price - Variable Costs)

B. (Selling Price - Variable Costs) / Fixed Costs

C. Fixed Costs × (Selling Price - Variable Costs)

D. (Selling Price - Variable Costs) × Fixed Costs

Answer: A

The break-even point is calculated by dividing fixed costs by the difference between the selling price and variable costs.

➡17. What is the formula for calculating the internal rate of return (IRR)?

A. $NPV = 0$

B. $ROI = 100\%$

C. $NPV \times ROI$

D. $ROI \times NPV$

Answer: A

The internal rate of return (IRR) is the discount rate that makes the net present value (NPV) of all cash flows equal to zero.

➡18. What is the formula for calculating the price per square foot?

A. Total Price / Total Square Footage

B. Total Square Footage / Total Price

C. Total Price × Total Square Footage

D. Total Square Footage × Total Price

Answer: A.

The price per square foot is calculated by dividing the total price by the total square footage.

➡19. What is the formula for calculating the amortization schedule?

A. $P \times (r(1+r)^n) / ((1+r)^n-1)$

B. $P \times r \times n$

C. $P / r \times n$

D. $P \times n / r$

Answer: A

The formula for calculating the amortization schedule is $P \times (r(1+r)^n) / ((1+r)^n - 1)$.

→20. What is the formula for calculating the future value of an investment?

A. $P \times (1 + r)^n$

B. $P \times (1 - r)^n$

C. $P / (1 + r)^n$

D. $P / (1 - r)^n$

Answer: A

The future value of an investment is calculated as $P \times (1 + r)^n$.

→21. How do you calculate the Net Operating Income (NOI) for a property?

A. Gross Income - Operating Expenses

B. Gross Income + Operating Expenses

C. Operating Expenses - Gross Income

D. Gross Income × Operating Expenses

Answer: A

Net Operating Income is calculated by subtracting the operating expenses from the gross income.

→22. What is the formula for calculating the loan-to-value ratio (LTV)?

A. Mortgage Amount / Appraised Value

B. Appraised Value / Mortgage Amount

C. Mortgage Amount × Appraised Value

D. Appraised Value × Mortgage Amount

Answer: A

The loan-to-value ratio (LTV) is calculated by dividing the mortgage amount by the appraised value of the property.

➡23. What is the formula for calculating the cash-on-cash return?

A. Annual Pre-tax Cash Flow / Total Cash Invested

B. Total Cash Invested / Annual Pre-tax Cash Flow

C. Annual Pre-tax Cash Flow × Total Cash Invested

D. Total Cash Invested × Annual Pre-tax Cash Flow

Answer: A

The cash-on-cash return is calculated by dividing the annual pre-tax cash flow by the total cash invested.

➡24. What is the formula for calculating the debt service coverage ratio (DSCR)?

A. Net Operating Income / Debt Service

B. Debt Service / Net Operating Income

C. Net Operating Income × Debt Service

D. Debt Service × Net Operating Income

Answer: A

The debt service coverage ratio (DSCR) is calculated by dividing the net operating income by the debt service.

➡25. What is the formula for calculating the equity build-up rate?

A. (Principal Paid in Year 1 / Initial Investment) × 100

B. (Initial Investment / Principal Paid in Year 1) × 100

C. Principal Paid in Year 1 × Initial Investment

D. Initial Investment × Principal Paid in Year 1

Answer: A

The equity build-up rate is calculated by dividing the principal paid in the first year by the initial investment and then multiplying by 100.

⟶26. What is the formula for calculating the gross operating income (GOI)?

A. Gross Potential Income - Vacancy and Credit Losses

B. Vacancy and Credit Losses - Gross Potential Income

C. Gross Potential Income × Vacancy and Credit Losses

D. Vacancy and Credit Losses × Gross Potential Income

Answer: A

The gross operating income (GOI) is calculated by subtracting vacancy and credit losses from the gross potential income.

⟶27. What is the formula for calculating the effective gross income (EGI)?

A. Gross Operating Income + Other Income

B. Other Income - Gross Operating Income

C. Gross Operating Income × Other Income

D. Other Income × Gross Operating Income

Answer: A

The effective gross income (EGI) is calculated by adding other income to the gross operating income.

⟶28. What is the formula for calculating the absorption rate?

A. Number of Units Sold / Number of Units Available

B. Number of Units Available / Number of Units Sold

C. Number of Units Sold × Number of Units Available

D. Number of Units Available × Number of Units Sold

Answer: A

The absorption rate is calculated by dividing the number of units sold by the number of units available.

➡ **29. What is the formula for calculating the price-to-rent ratio?**

A. Home Price / Annual Rent

B. Annual Rent / Home Price

C. Home Price × Annual Rent

D. Annual Rent × Home Price

Answer: A

The price-to-rent ratio is calculated by dividing the home price by the annual rent.

➡ **30. What is the formula for calculating the yield?**

A. Annual Income / Investment Cost

B. Investment Cost / Annual Income

C. Annual Income × Investment Cost

D. Investment Cost × Annual Income

Answer: A

The yield is calculated by dividing the annual income by the investment cost.

➡ **31. What is the formula for calculating the Gross Rent Multiplier (GRM)?**

A. Sales Price / Monthly Rent

B. Monthly Rent / Sales Price

C. Sales Price × Monthly Rent

D. Monthly Rent × Sales Price

Answer: A

The Gross Rent Multiplier (GRM) is calculated by dividing the sales price by the monthly rent.

➡️**32. How do you calculate the Loan-to-Value ratio (LTV)?**

A. Loan Amount / Appraised Value

B. Appraised Value / Loan Amount

C. Loan Amount × Appraised Value

D. Appraised Value × Loan Amount

Answer: A

The Loan-to-Value ratio (LTV) is calculated by dividing the loan amount by the appraised value of the property.

➡️**33. How do you calculate the Net Operating Income (NOI)?**

A. Gross Operating Income - Operating Expenses

B. Operating Expenses - Gross Operating Income

C. Gross Operating Income × Operating Expenses

D. Operating Expenses × Gross Operating Income

Answer: A

The Net Operating Income (NOI) is calculated by subtracting the operating expenses from the gross operating income.

➡️**34. How do you calculate the Debt Service Coverage Ratio (DSCR)?**

A. Net Operating Income / Debt Service

B. Debt Service / Net Operating Income

C. Net Operating Income × Debt Service

D. Debt Service × Net Operating Income

Answer: A

The Debt Service Coverage Ratio (DSCR) is calculated by dividing the Net Operating Income by the Debt Service.

➡35. What is the formula for calculating the Break-Even Ratio (BER)?

A. (Operating Expenses + Debt Service) / Gross Operating Income

B. Gross Operating Income / (Operating Expenses + Debt Service)

C. (Operating Expenses + Debt Service) × Gross Operating Income

D. Gross Operating Income × (Operating Expenses + Debt Service)

Answer: A

The Break-Even Ratio (BER) is calculated by dividing the sum of operating expenses and debt service by the gross operating income.

➡36. How do you calculate the Effective Gross Income (EGI)?

A. Gross Income - Vacancy Losses + Other Income

B. Gross Income + Vacancy Losses - Other Income

C. Gross Income × Vacancy Losses + Other Income

D. Gross Income + Vacancy Losses × Other Income

Answer: A

The Effective Gross Income (EGI) is calculated by subtracting vacancy losses from the gross income and adding any other income.

➡37. What is the formula for calculating the Operating Expense Ratio (OER)?

A. Operating Expenses / Effective Gross Income

B. Effective Gross Income / Operating Expenses

C. Operating Expenses × Effective Gross Income

D. Effective Gross Income × Operating Expenses

Answer: A

The Operating Expense Ratio (OER) is calculated by dividing the operating expenses by the effective gross income.

➡**38. How do you calculate the Cash-on-Cash Return?**

A. Cash Flow Before Taxes / Initial Investment

B. Initial Investment / Cash Flow Before Taxes

C. Cash Flow Before Taxes × Initial Investment

D. Initial Investment × Cash Flow Before Taxes

Answer: A

The Cash-on-Cash Return is calculated by dividing the cash flow before taxes by the initial investment.

➡**39. What is the formula for calculating the Amortization Factor?**

A. Monthly Payment / Loan Amount

B. Loan Amount / Monthly Payment

C. Monthly Payment × Loan Amount

D. Loan Amount × Monthly Payment

Answer: A

The Amortization Factor is calculated by dividing the monthly payment by the loan amount.

➡**40. How do you calculate the Equity Dividend Rate (EDR)?**

A. Cash Flow After Taxes / Equity Investment

B. Equity Investment / Cash Flow After Taxes

C. Cash Flow After Taxes × Equity Investment

D. Equity Investment × Cash Flow After Taxes

➡41. What is the formula for calculating the Debt Service Coverage Ratio (DSCR)?

A. Net Operating Income / Debt Service

B. Debt Service / Net Operating Income

C. Net Operating Income × Debt Service

D. Debt Service - Net Operating Income

Answer: A

The Debt Service Coverage Ratio is calculated by dividing the Net Operating Income by the Debt Service.

➡42. How do you calculate the Gross Rent Multiplier (GRM)?

A. Property Price / Monthly Rent

B. Monthly Rent / Property Price

C. Annual Rent / Property Price

D. Property Price / Annual Rent

Answer: A

The Gross Rent Multiplier is calculated by dividing the property price by the monthly rent.

➡43. What is the formula for calculating Loan-to-Value ratio?

A. Loan Amount / Property Value

B. Property Value / Loan Amount

C. Loan Amount × Property Value

D. Property Value - Loan Amount

Answer: A

The Loan-to-Value ratio is calculated by dividing the loan amount by the property value.

➡44. How do you calculate the break-even point in a real estate investment?

   A. Fixed Costs / (Selling Price - Variable Costs)

   B. (Selling Price - Variable Costs) / Fixed Costs

   C. Fixed Costs × Selling Price

   D. Selling Price / Fixed Costs

Answer: A

The break-even point is calculated by dividing the fixed costs by the difference between the selling price and variable costs.

➡45. How do you calculate the Return on Investment (ROI) for a property?

   A. (Net Profit / Investment Cost) × 100

   B. (Investment Cost / Net Profit) × 100

   C. Net Profit × Investment Cost

   D. Investment Cost - Net Profit

Answer: A

The Return on Investment is calculated by dividing the net profit by the investment cost and then multiplying by 100.

➡46. How do you calculate the equity in a property?

   A. Property Value - Mortgage Balance

   B. Mortgage Balance - Property Value

   C. Property Value × Mortgage Balance

   D. Mortgage Balance / Property Value

Answer: A

Equity is calculated by subtracting the mortgage balance from the property value.

➡ **47. What is the formula for calculating the amortization payment?**

   A. Principal Amount / Number of Payments

   B. Interest Rate / Number of Payments

   C. (Principal Amount × Interest Rate) / Number of Payments

   D. (Principal Amount × Interest Rate) / (1 - (1 + Interest Rate)^-Number of Payments)

Answer: D

The amortization payment is calculated using the formula mentioned.

➡ **48. What is the formula for calculating the Internal Rate of Return (IRR) for a real estate investment?**

   A. The discount rate that makes the Net Present Value zero

   B. The rate that equals the Net Operating Income

   C. The rate that equals the Debt Service

   D. The rate that makes the Gross Income zero

Answer: A

The Internal Rate of Return is the discount rate that makes the Net Present Value of all cash flows from a particular investment equal to zero.

➡ **49. What is the formula for calculating the rate of return on an investment property?**

   A. (Net Profit / Cost of Investment) × 100

   B. (Cost of Investment / Net Profit) × 100

   C. Net Profit × Cost of Investment

D. Cost of Investment - Net Profit

Answer: A

The rate of return is calculated by dividing the net profit by the cost of the investment and then multiplying by 100.

➡️**50. How do you calculate the net profit from a real estate investment?**

    A. Selling Price - (Buying Price + Costs)

    B. (Buying Price + Costs) - Selling Price

    C. Selling Price × Buying Price

    D. Buying Price / Selling Price

Answer: A

The Net Operating Income (NOI) is calculated by subtracting the operating expenses from the gross operating income.

Specialty Areas

The real estate industry is a vast and diverse field, offering numerous specialty areas that cater to different market segments, property types, and client needs. In Washington State, the real estate landscape is particularly varied, thanks to its unique geography, economy, and demographic makeup. This chapter aims to provide an in-depth look into the various specialty areas within the Washington real estate market, offering valuable insights for both aspiring and seasoned professionals.

Residential Real Estate

Single-Family Homes

The most common type of residential real estate, single-family homes are standalone houses that offer privacy and independence. They are prevalent in suburban areas and are often the first choice for families.

Condominiums

Condominiums are individual units within a larger building or complex. They offer a sense of community and often come with amenities like swimming pools and gyms.

Townhouses

These are multi-level homes that share one or more walls with adjacent properties. They offer a middle ground between single-family homes and condominiums.

Vacation Homes

Washington's scenic beauty makes it a popular location for vacation homes, especially near tourist destinations like the San Juan Islands and Lake Chelan.

Commercial Real Estate

Office Spaces

The demand for office spaces is high in cities like Seattle, which is a hub for tech companies and startups.

Retail Spaces

From shopping malls to individual storefronts, retail spaces are a significant part of Washington's commercial real estate.

Industrial Properties

These include warehouses, factories, and distribution centers. The ports in Seattle and Tacoma make industrial real estate a lucrative investment.

Investment Real Estate

Rental Properties

Owning rental properties can provide a steady income stream. This could be residential rentals or vacation rentals.

Real Estate Investment Trusts (REITs)

These are companies that own or finance income-producing real estate across various property sectors.

Luxury Real Estate

Washington has a thriving luxury real estate market, especially in areas like Bellevue and Mercer Island. These properties often come with high-end amenities and are located in prime locations.

Farm and Land

Agricultural Real Estate

Washington is known for its diverse agricultural output, including apples, hops, and wine grapes. Agricultural real estate can be a rewarding but challenging specialty.

Timberland

With its vast forests, timberland is another unique real estate investment opportunity in Washington.

Historic and Architectural Real Estate

Preserving historic homes and buildings is a niche but growing field. It requires specialized knowledge of restoration techniques and historical architecture.

Green and Sustainable Real Estate

With a strong focus on sustainability, Washington is a leader in green building practices. This specialty area focuses on energy-efficient homes and commercial spaces.

Legal and Regulatory Considerations

Each specialty area comes with its own set of laws and regulations. For example, agricultural land may have zoning restrictions, and commercial properties might require specific permits.

Ethical Considerations

Regardless of the specialty area, real estate professionals must adhere to ethical standards, including honesty, integrity, and full disclosure.

Career Opportunities

Specializing in a particular area can open up new career opportunities and allow you to become an expert in that field. It may also lead to higher commissions and a more targeted client base.

Conclusion

The real estate industry in Washington State offers a plethora of specialty areas to explore. Whether you're interested in residential, commercial, or something more niche like historic or green real estate, there's something for everyone. Understanding the unique characteristics, legal frameworks, and market demands of these specialty areas can provide a significant advantage in your real estate career.

Mock Exam Specialty Areas

→1. Which type of real estate is often the entry point for many new agents and brokers?

    A. Commercial

    B. Industrial

    C. Residential

    D. Luxury

Answer: C. Residential

Explanation: The chapter states that residential real estate is often the entry point for many new agents and brokers.

→2. What type of property is a penthouse?

    A. Industrial

    B. Commercial

    C. Residential

    D. Luxury

Answer: D. Luxury

Explanation: Penthouses are high-end apartments located on the top floors of high-rise buildings and fall under luxury real estate.

→3. What is a key skill required in commercial real estate?

    A. Financial Analysis

    B. Knowledge of Industrial Machinery

    C. Strong Interpersonal Skills

    D. Discretion and Confidentiality

Answer: A. Financial Analysis

Explanation: Financial analysis is crucial in commercial real estate for understanding balance sheets, income statements, and cash flow.

➡4. What type of property is a factory?

A. Commercial

B. Industrial

C. Residential

D. Luxury

Answer: B. Industrial

Explanation: Factories are geared towards manufacturing, production, and distribution, which falls under industrial real estate.

➡5. What is a key regulatory aspect in industrial real estate?

A. Luxury tax implications

B. OSHA regulations

C. Fair Housing Laws

D. Commercial zoning laws

Answer: B. OSHA regulations

Explanation: Occupational Safety and Health Administration (OSHA) regulations are key in industrial real estate.

➡6. What type of property is a shopping mall?

A. Commercial

B. Industrial

C. Residential

D. Luxury

Answer: A. Commercial

Explanation: Shopping malls fall under commercial real estate as they are used for business activities.

➡7. **What is a key skill required in luxury real estate?**

A. Financial Analysis

B. Knowledge of Industrial Machinery

C. Strong Interpersonal Skills

D. Discretion and Confidentiality

Answer: D. Discretion and Confidentiality

Explanation: Clients in the luxury sector value their privacy highly, making discretion and confidentiality key skills.

➡8. **What type of property is a townhouse?**

A. Commercial

B. Industrial

C. Residential

D. Luxury

Answer: C. Residential

Explanation: Townhouses are multi-floor homes designed for individual or family living, which falls under residential real estate.

➡9. **What is a key regulatory aspect in residential real estate?**

A. Luxury tax implications

B. OSHA regulations

C. Fair Housing Laws

D. Commercial zoning laws

Answer: C. Fair Housing Laws

Explanation: Fair Housing Laws are key regulatory aspects in residential real estate to ensure equal opportunity in housing.

➡10. **What type of property is a distribution center?**

A. Commercial

B. Industrial

C. Residential

D. Luxury

Answer: B. Industrial

Explanation: Distribution centers are used for storing and distributing goods, which falls under industrial real estate.

➡11. **What type of real estate involves the sale of businesses?**

A. Commercial

B. Business Brokerage

C. Residential

D. Luxury

Answer: B. Business Brokerage

Explanation: Business Brokerage involves the sale of businesses, including their assets and real estate.

➡12. **What is a key skill required in business brokerage?**

A. Negotiation Skills

B. Knowledge of Industrial Machinery

C. Strong Interpersonal Skills

D. Financial Analysis

Answer: A. Negotiation Skills

Explanation: Negotiation skills are crucial in business brokerage to secure the best deals for clients.

➡️**13. What type of real estate involves the sale of farmland?**

A. Commercial

B. Industrial

C. Agricultural

D. Luxury

Answer: C. Agricultural

Explanation: Agricultural real estate involves the sale of farmland and agricultural facilities.

➡️**14. What is a key regulatory aspect in agricultural real estate?**

A. EPA Regulations

B. OSHA regulations

C. Fair Housing Laws

D. Luxury tax implications

Answer: A. EPA Regulations

Explanation: Environmental Protection Agency (EPA) regulations are key in agricultural real estate.

→ **15. What type of property is a hotel?**

A. Commercial

B. Industrial

C. Residential

D. Hospitality

Answer: D. Hospitality

Explanation: Hotels fall under hospitality real estate, which is a sub-category of commercial real estate.

→ **16. What is a key skill required in hospitality real estate?**

A. Customer Service

B. Knowledge of Industrial Machinery

C. Strong Interpersonal Skills

D. Financial Analysis

Answer: A. Customer Service

Explanation: Customer service is crucial in hospitality real estate to ensure guest satisfaction.

→ **17. What type of real estate involves the sale of undeveloped land?**

A. Commercial

B. Land

C. Residential

D. Luxury

Answer: B. Land

Explanation: The sale of undeveloped land falls under land real estate.

→ **18. What is a key regulatory aspect in land real estate?**

A. Zoning Laws

B. OSHA regulations

C. Fair Housing Laws

D. Luxury tax implications

Answer: A. Zoning Laws

Explanation: Zoning laws are key in land real estate to determine the types of development that can occur.

➡19. **What type of property is a condominium?**

A. Commercial

B. Industrial

C. Residential

D. Luxury

Answer: C. Residential

Explanation: Condominiums are multi-unit properties that are sold individually, which falls under residential real estate.

➡20. **What is a key skill required in land real estate?**

A. Negotiation Skills

B. Knowledge of Zoning Laws

C. Strong Interpersonal Skills

D. Financial Analysis

Answer: B. Knowledge of Zoning Laws

Explanation: Knowledge of zoning laws is crucial in land real estate to guide clients on permissible uses.

→21. What is the primary focus of industrial real estate?

A. Warehouses

B. Hotels

C. Farmland

D. Condominiums

Answer: A. Warehouses

Explanation: Industrial real estate primarily focuses on warehouses and manufacturing buildings.

→22. What is a 1031 exchange commonly used for?

A. Residential properties

B. Commercial properties

C. Agricultural properties

D. Industrial properties

Answer: B. Commercial properties

Explanation: A 1031 exchange is commonly used to defer capital gains tax in commercial real estate.

→23. What is the main consideration in retail real estate?

A. Location

B. Size

C. Zoning

D. Tax implications

Answer: A. Location

Explanation: Location is the main consideration in retail real estate, as it directly impacts customer footfall.

➡ **24. What is the primary focus of residential real estate?**

A. Single-family homes

B. Warehouses

C. Hotels

D. Farmland

Answer: **A. Single-family homes**

Explanation: Residential real estate primarily focuses on single-family homes, although it can include multi-family units.

➡ **25. What is the main consideration in luxury real estate?**

A. Price

B. Location

C. Amenities

D. Size

Answer: **C. Amenities**

Explanation: Luxury real estate often focuses on the amenities offered, such as pools, gyms, and concierge services.

➡ **26. What is the primary advantage of investing in mixed-use real estate?**

A. Diversification

B. Lower taxes

C. Easier management

D. Higher rent

Answer: **A. Diversification**

Explanation: Mixed-use real estate offers diversification as it combines residential, commercial, and sometimes industrial spaces.

→27. What is the main disadvantage of investing in vacation real estate?

A. Seasonal income

B. High maintenance

C. Zoning restrictions

D. High taxes

Answer: A. Seasonal income

Explanation: Vacation real estate often has seasonal income, which can be a disadvantage for consistent cash flow.

→28. What is the primary consideration when investing in student housing?

A. Proximity to educational institutions

B. Luxury amenities

C. Tax benefits

D. Size of the property

Answer: A. Proximity to educational institutions

Explanation: The primary consideration for student housing is its proximity to educational institutions.

→29. What is the main benefit of investing in senior living communities?

A. Lower maintenance

B. Steady income

C. Tax benefits

D. High rent

Answer: B. Steady income

Explanation: Senior living communities often provide a steady income due to long-term leases.

➡️30. What is a triple net lease commonly used in?

A. Residential properties

B. Commercial properties

C. Industrial properties

D. Agricultural properties

Answer: B. Commercial properties

Explanation: A triple net lease is commonly used in commercial real estate, where the tenant pays property taxes, insurance, and maintenance costs.

➡️31. What is the primary focus of hospitality real estate?

A. Hotels and resorts

B. Warehouses

C. Office buildings

D. Farmland

Answer: A. Hotels and resorts

Explanation: Hospitality real estate primarily focuses on hotels, resorts, and other lodging options.

➡️32. What is the main consideration in agricultural real estate?

A. Soil quality

B. Location

C. Size

D. Zoning

Answer: A. Soil quality

Explanation: Soil quality is the main consideration in agricultural real estate for farming purposes.

➡33. What is the primary advantage of investing in REITs?

A. Liquidity

B. Control over property

C. Tax benefits

D. High rent

Answer: A. Liquidity

Explanation: REITs offer liquidity as they can be easily bought and sold on stock exchanges.

➡34. What is the main disadvantage of investing in office real estate?

A. High vacancy rates

B. Seasonal income

C. Zoning restrictions

D. High maintenance

Answer: A. High vacancy rates

Explanation: Office real estate can have high vacancy rates, especially in economic downturns.

➡35. What is the primary focus of mobile home parks?

A. Affordable housing

B. Luxury living

C. Commercial spaces

D. Agricultural land

Answer: A. Affordable housing

Explanation: Mobile home parks primarily focus on providing affordable housing options.

➡36. What is the primary consideration when investing in retail real estate?

A. Foot traffic

B. Tax benefits

C. Size of the property

D. Proximity to educational institutions

Answer: A. Foot traffic

Explanation: Foot traffic is crucial for the success of retail real estate.

➡37. What is the main benefit of investing in industrial real estate?

A. High rent

B. Long-term leases

C. Seasonal income

D. Tax benefits

Answer: B. Long-term leases

Explanation: Industrial real estate often comes with long-term leases, providing stable income.

➡38. What is a common disadvantage of investing in multi-family properties?

A. High maintenance costs

B. Low rent

C. Zoning restrictions

D. Seasonal income

Answer: A. High maintenance costs

Explanation: Multi-family properties often have higher maintenance costs due to multiple units.

➡39. What is the primary focus of medical real estate?

A. Hospitals and clinics

B. Office buildings

C. Warehouses

D. Hotels and resorts

Answer: A. Hospitals and clinics

Explanation: Medical real estate primarily focuses on hospitals, clinics, and other healthcare facilities.

➡40. What is the main consideration in raw land investment?

A. Zoning restrictions

B. Soil quality

C. Location

D. Size

Answer: C. Location

Explanation: Location is key in raw land investment for future development.

➡41. What is the primary advantage of investing in storage units?

A. Low maintenance

B. High rent

C. Tax benefits

D. Seasonal income

Answer: A. Low maintenance

Explanation: Storage units generally require low maintenance.

➡42. What is the main disadvantage of investing in co-working spaces?

A. High vacancy rates

B. Low rent

C. Zoning restrictions

D. Seasonal income

Answer: A. High vacancy rates

Explanation: Co-working spaces can have high vacancy rates, especially during economic downturns.

➡43. What is the primary focus of green real estate?

A. Energy efficiency

B. High rent

C. Tax benefits

D. Size of the property

Answer: A. Energy efficiency

Explanation: Green real estate primarily focuses on energy-efficient buildings.

➡44. What is the main benefit of investing in brownfield sites?

A. Tax incentives

B. High rent

C. Seasonal income

D. Long-term leases

Answer: A. Tax incentives

Explanation: Brownfield sites often come with tax incentives for redevelopment.

➡45. What is the primary consideration when investing in infill real estate?

A. Location

B. Size

C. Zoning restrictions

D. Soil quality

Answer: **A. Location**

Explanation: Infill real estate focuses on developing vacant or underused parcels within existing urban areas, so location is key.

➡46. What is the main disadvantage of investing in luxury real estate?

A. High maintenance costs

B. Seasonal income

C. Zoning restrictions

D. Low rent

Answer: **A. High maintenance costs**

Explanation: Luxury real estate often comes with high maintenance costs.

➡47. What is the primary focus of transit-oriented development?

A. Proximity to public transport

B. Luxury amenities

C. Tax benefits

D. Size of the property

Answer: **A. Proximity to public transport**

Explanation: Transit-oriented development focuses on properties close to public transport facilities.

➡48. What is the main benefit of investing in adaptive reuse properties?

A. Tax incentives

B. High rent

C. Seasonal income

D. Long-term leases

Answer: A. Tax incentives

Explanation: Adaptive reuse properties often come with tax incentives for redevelopment.

➡49. What is the primary consideration when investing in distressed properties?

A. Cost of renovation

B. Location

C. Size

D. Zoning

Answer: A. Cost of renovation

Explanation: The cost of renovation is a key consideration when investing in distressed properties.

➡50. What is the main disadvantage of investing in fixer-uppers?

A. High renovation costs

B. Low rent

C. Zoning restrictions

D. Seasonal income

Answer: A. High renovation costs

Explanation: Fixer-uppers often come with high renovation costs that can eat into profits.

Ethics and Legal Considerations

Ethics and legal considerations are the bedrock of any profession, and real estate is no exception. In Washington State, real estate professionals are bound by a set of ethical guidelines and legal obligations that govern their interactions with clients, colleagues, and the broader community. This chapter delves into the intricacies of these ethical and legal considerations, providing a comprehensive guide for both aspiring and experienced real estate professionals in Washington.

Ethical Guidelines

Code of Ethics

The National Association of Realtors (NAR) provides a Code of Ethics that serves as the industry standard. In Washington, the Washington Realtors association also has its own set of ethical guidelines that align with NAR's principles.

Fiduciary Duty

Real estate agents have a fiduciary duty to their clients, meaning they must act in the best interests of their clients at all times. This includes confidentiality, full disclosure, and the duty to put the client's needs above their own.

Honesty and Integrity

Agents are expected to conduct all business with honesty and integrity, which includes not misleading clients or providing false information.

Fair Housing and Discrimination

Federal and state laws prohibit discrimination based on race, color, religion, sex, disability, familial status, or national origin. Washington State also includes sexual orientation, marital status, and military status as protected classes.

Legal Considerations

Licensing Requirements

In Washington, real estate professionals must be licensed by the Washington State Department of Licensing. This involves passing an exam and fulfilling continuing education requirements.

Contract Law

Real estate transactions are bound by contract law, which stipulates the obligations of each party. Agents must ensure that contracts are legally sound and understood by all parties.

Disclosure Requirements

Washington State law requires sellers to provide a detailed disclosure form to buyers, outlining any known issues with the property. Failure to disclose can result in legal repercussions.

Zoning and Land Use Laws

Real estate professionals must be aware of local zoning laws, which can affect property usage. This is especially important in specialty areas like agricultural or commercial real estate.

Data Privacy

With the advent of digital technology, safeguarding client data has become a legal obligation. Washington State has specific laws governing data protection and privacy.

Case Studies

Case Study 1: Breach of Fiduciary Duty

In this case, an agent prioritized their own financial gain over the best interests of the client, leading to a lawsuit and loss of license.

Case Study 2: Fair Housing Violation

An agent was found guilty of steering minority clients away from certain neighborhoods, resulting in a Fair Housing Act violation and severe penalties.

Case Study 3: Failure to Disclose

A seller, advised by their agent, failed to disclose a major structural issue with the property. The buyer sued both the seller and the agent for damages.

Risk Management

Professional Liability Insurance

Also known as Errors and Omissions (E&O) insurance, this protects agents from legal claims or disputes.

Record-Keeping

Maintaining accurate and complete records can serve as a defense in legal disputes and is a requirement under Washington State law.

Continuing Education

Staying updated on legal changes and ethical guidelines is crucial. Washington requires ongoing education for license renewal.

Conclusion

Ethics and legal considerations are not just guidelines but are crucial for the long-term success and credibility of real estate professionals. In Washington, these principles are governed by a mix of federal and state laws, industry standards, and ethical codes. Adherence to these not only fulfills legal obligations but also builds trust, which is the cornerstone of any successful real estate career.

By understanding and implementing these ethical and legal considerations, you are not just complying with the law; you are elevating the entire profession. This chapter serves as a comprehensive guide, but it's essential to consult legal advisors and stay updated on the latest changes in laws and ethics.

Mock Exam Ethics and Legal Considerations

➡1. What are the three main categories of the NAR Code of Ethics?

A. Duties to Clients, Duties to Realtors, Duties to the Public

B. Duties to Clients and Customers, Duties to the Public, Duties to Realtors

C. Duties to Sellers, Duties to Buyers, Duties to the Public

D. Duties to the Government, Duties to Clients, Duties to Realtors

Answer: B

The NAR Code of Ethics is divided into three main categories: Duties to Clients and Customers, Duties to the Public, and Duties to Realtors.

➡2. Which of the following is NOT a fiduciary duty?

A. Loyalty

B. Confidentiality

C. Manipulation

D. Full Disclosure

Answer: C

Manipulation is not a fiduciary duty. The fiduciary duties are loyalty, confidentiality, obedience, reasonable care, accounting, and full disclosure.

➡3. What is the primary purpose of zoning laws?

A. To increase property taxes

B. To regulate land use

C. To protect endangered species

D. To promote business

Answer: B

The primary purpose of zoning laws is to regulate land use, such as residential, commercial, or industrial zones.

➡4. What does 'reasonable care' in fiduciary duties imply?

    A. Taking vacations regularly

    B. Staying updated on market trends

    C. Investing in real estate

    D. Focusing on commission

Answer: B

'Reasonable care' means staying updated on market trends, legal changes, and other factors that could affect a client's decision.

➡5. What is the consequence of not adhering to full disclosure?

    A. Increased commission

    B. Legal repercussions

    C. More clients

    D. Promotion

Answer: B

Failing to adhere to full disclosure can lead to legal repercussions, including lawsuits and loss of license.

➡6. Which federal law is designed to ensure fair housing?

    A. The Sherman Act

    B. The Fair Housing Act

    C. The Clayton Act

    D. The Dodd-Frank Act

Answer: B

The Fair Housing Act is designed to prevent discrimination in housing based on race, color, religion, sex, or national origin.

➥7. What is the minimum age requirement for obtaining a real estate license in most states?

A. 16

B. 18

C. 21

D. 25

Answer: B

The minimum age requirement for obtaining a real estate license in most states is 18 years.

➥8. What is the key to resolving ethical dilemmas like dual agency?

A. Ignoring the issue

B. Full disclosure and informed consent

C. Choosing one party to represent

D. Consulting a lawyer

Answer: B

The key to resolving ethical dilemmas like dual agency lies in full disclosure and obtaining informed consent from all parties involved.

➥9. Which of the following is NOT an element that makes a contract legally binding?

A. Offer and acceptance

B. Consideration

C. Coercion

D. Legality of purpose

Answer: C

Coercion is not an element that makes a contract legally binding. A contract must have offer and acceptance, consideration, and legality of purpose to be legally binding.

➡10. What does the NAR Code of Ethics say about advertising?

A. It encourages aggressive advertising

B. It prohibits all forms of advertising

C. It requires truthful advertising

D. It promotes online advertising only

Answer: C

The NAR Code of Ethics requires that all advertising be truthful and not misleading.

➡11. What is the primary role of the Real Estate Commission in most states?

A. To sell properties

B. To regulate and license real estate agents

C. To build homes

D. To provide loans

Answer: B

The primary role of the Real Estate Commission in most states is to regulate and license real estate agents.

➡12. What is the statute of frauds?

A. A law that requires certain contracts to be in writing

B. A law that allows fraud in certain cases

C. A law that regulates online advertising

D. A law that deals with zoning issues

Answer: A

The statute of frauds is a law that requires certain contracts, like those for the sale of real estate, to be in writing to be enforceable.

➡️13. What does RESPA stand for?

A. Real Estate Settlement Procedures Act

B. Real Estate Sales Professional Act

C. Residential Sales Property Act

D. Real Estate Security Policy Act

Answer: A

RESPA stands for Real Estate Settlement Procedures Act, which aims to provide transparency in the home buying process.

➡️14. What is puffing in real estate terms?

A. Illegal misrepresentation

B. Exaggeration of property features

C. Accurate description of property

D. Undervaluing a property

Answer: B

Puffing refers to the exaggeration of property features, which is generally considered legal but can be ethically questionable.

➡️15. What is the primary purpose of an escrow account?

A. To hold funds for investment

B. To hold funds until the completion of a real estate transaction

C. To pay for the agent's commission

D. To pay property taxes

Answer: B

The primary purpose of an escrow account is to hold funds until the completion of a real estate transaction.

➡16. What does the term "redlining" refer to?

A. Drawing property boundaries

B. Discriminatory lending practices

C. Marking properties for demolition

D. Highlighting important clauses in a contract

Answer: B

Redlining refers to discriminatory lending practices that deny loans or insurance to people based on their location, often targeting minority communities.

➡17. What is the difference between ethics and laws?

A. Ethics are legally binding, laws are not

B. Laws are legally binding, ethics are not

C. Ethics and laws are the same

D. Laws are optional, ethics are mandatory

Answer: B

Laws are legally binding rules that must be followed, while ethics are moral principles that guide behavior but are not legally enforceable.

→18. What is the "doctrine of caveat emptor"?

A. Let the buyer beware

B. Let the seller beware

C. Buyer's premium

D. Seller's advantage

Answer: A

The doctrine of "caveat emptor" means "let the buyer beware," indicating that the buyer is responsible for due diligence.

→19. What is a bilateral contract?

A. A contract with only one party

B. A contract with two parties

C. A contract with multiple parties

D. A contract that is not legally binding

Answer: B

A bilateral contract is a contract involving two parties where each party has made a promise to the other.

→20. What is the role of a title company?

A. To market properties

B. To ensure the title is clear and prepare for its transfer

C. To provide loans

D. To build homes

Answer: B

The role of a title company is to ensure that the title to a piece of real estate is legitimate and to prepare for its transfer from the seller to the buyer.

→21. What is the "dual agency" in real estate?

A. When an agent represents both the buyer and the seller

B. When two agents work for the same client

C. When an agent works for two different real estate firms

D. When an agent sells both commercial and residential properties

Answer: A

Dual agency occurs when a real estate agent represents both the buyer and the seller in the same transaction.

→22. What does the Fair Housing Act prohibit?

A. Discrimination based on race, color, religion, sex, or national origin

B. All forms of discrimination

C. Discrimination based on financial status

D. Discrimination based on occupation

Answer: A

The Fair Housing Act prohibits discrimination in housing based on race, color, religion, sex, or national origin.

→23. What is earnest money?

A. Money paid by the buyer at the time of the property closing

B. A refundable deposit

C. Money paid by the buyer to show serious intent to purchase

D. Money paid by the seller as a part of the listing agreement

Answer: C

Earnest money is money paid by the buyer to show serious intent to purchase the property.

➡24. What is a contingency in a real estate contract?

A. A binding clause

B. A non-negotiable term

C. A condition that must be met for the contract to be binding

D. A penalty for breach of contract

Answer: C

A contingency is a condition that must be met for the contract to be binding, such as a home inspection.

➡25. What is a fiduciary duty?

A. A legal obligation to act in the best interest of another

B. A duty to find the best property for a client

C. A duty to sell a property as quickly as possible

D. A duty to maximize profit

Answer: A

A fiduciary duty is a legal obligation to act in the best interest of another, such as a client.

➡26. What is a unilateral contract?

A. A contract where only one party makes a promise

B. A contract where both parties make promises

C. A contract that involves more than two parties

D. A contract that is not legally binding

Answer: A

A unilateral contract is a contract where only one party makes a promise, and the other has the option to complete the action.

→27. What is the purpose of a disclosure statement?

A. To disclose the agent's commission

B. To disclose any known defects or issues with the property

C. To disclose the buyer's financial status

D. To disclose the terms of the mortgage

Answer: B

The purpose of a disclosure statement is to disclose any known defects or issues with the property to the buyer.

→28. What does "time is of the essence" mean in a real estate contract?

A. Deadlines must be strictly adhered to

B. Time limits are flexible

C. The contract has no expiration date

D. The contract can be terminated at any time

Answer: A

"Time is of the essence" means that deadlines set forth in the contract must be strictly adhered to.

→29. What is a quitclaim deed?

A. A deed that transfers property with no warranties

B. A deed that includes warranties

C. A deed that transfers leasehold interest

D. A deed that can be easily revoked

Answer: A

A quitclaim deed is a deed that transfers property with no warranties or guarantees.

➡ **30. What is the role of a notary public in a real estate transaction?**

A. To negotiate the terms

B. To verify the identity of the parties and witness the signing of documents

C. To provide legal advice

D. To inspect the property

Answer: B

The role of a notary public is to verify the identity of the parties and witness the signing of important documents.

➡ **31. What is the primary purpose of a title search?**

A. To determine the property's market value

B. To verify the legal owner of the property

C. To inspect the condition of the property

D. To assess property taxes

Answer: B

The primary purpose of a title search is to verify the legal owner of the property and ensure there are no liens or other encumbrances.

➡ **32. What is a "balloon payment" in a mortgage?**

A. A small initial payment

B. A large final payment

C. A regular monthly payment

D. An extra payment to reduce interest

Answer: B

A balloon payment is a large final payment at the end of a loan term, usually after a series of smaller payments.

➟**33. What is the "right of first refusal" in real estate?**

A. The right to refuse a sale

B. The right to be the first to purchase a property before the owner sells it to another party

C. The right to refuse to pay rent

D. The right to refuse a home inspection

Answer: B

The right of first refusal allows an individual or entity the opportunity to purchase a property before the owner sells it to another party.

➟**34. What is a "listing agreement"?**

A. An agreement between buyer and seller

B. An agreement between a seller and a real estate agent

C. An agreement between a buyer and a real estate agent

D. An agreement between two real estate agents

Answer: B

A listing agreement is a contract between a seller and a real estate agent outlining the terms under which the agent will sell the property.

➟**35. What does "under contract" mean in real estate?**

A. The property is being appraised

B. The property is being inspected

C. An offer on the property has been accepted, but the sale is not yet complete

D. The property has been sold

Answer: C

"Under contract" means that an offer on the property has been accepted, but the sale is not yet complete, pending contingencies or other terms.

➠**36. What is the role of a fiduciary in a real estate transaction?**

    A. To act in the best interest of the client

    B. To maximize profits for the brokerage

    C. To represent both buyer and seller equally

    D. To ensure the property passes inspection

Answer: A

The role of a fiduciary is to act in the best interest of the client, whether that's the buyer or the seller.

➠**37. What does "escrow" refer to in real estate?**

    A. A type of mortgage loan

    B. A neutral third party holding funds or documents until conditions are met

    C. A binding contract between buyer and seller

    D. A home inspection report

Answer: B

Escrow refers to a neutral third party holding funds or documents until certain conditions are met in a real estate transaction.

➠**38. What is a "contingency" in a real estate contract?**

    A. A penalty for late payment

    B. A condition that must be met for the contract to proceed

    C. An optional add-on to the property

D. A mandatory fee paid to the real estate agent

Answer: B

A contingency is a condition that must be met for the contract to proceed, such as a successful home inspection.

➡ **39. What does "amortization" mean in the context of a mortgage?**

A. The process of increasing the loan amount

B. The process of paying off the loan over time

C. The process of adjusting the interest rate

D. The process of transferring the loan to another lender

Answer: B

Amortization is the process of paying off a loan over time through regular payments.

➡ **40. What is "due diligence" in real estate?**

A. The responsibility to investigate a property before purchase

B. The obligation to pay property taxes

C. The requirement to obtain a mortgage pre-approval

D. The duty to disclose all known defects to a buyer

Answer: A

Due diligence is the responsibility of the buyer to investigate a property thoroughly before completing the purchase.

➡ **41. What is "redlining" in the context of real estate?**

A. Drawing property boundaries

B. Discriminatory practice affecting mortgage availability

C. A type of home inspection

D. A negotiation strategy

Answer: B

Redlining is a discriminatory practice where mortgage lenders deny loans or insurance to certain areas based on racial or ethnic composition.

➡ **42. What does "title insurance" protect against?**

A. Property damage

B. Mortgage default

C. Legal claims against property ownership

D. Loss of rental income

Answer: C

Title insurance protects against legal claims challenging the ownership of the property.

➡ **43. What is "dual agency" in real estate?**

A. When an agent represents both the buyer and the seller

B. When two agents from the same brokerage represent the buyer and the seller

C. When an agent represents two buyers for the same property

D. When an agent represents two sellers for different properties

Answer: A

Dual agency occurs when a real estate agent represents both the buyer and the seller in the same transaction. This can create a conflict of interest and is illegal in some states.

➡ **44. What is a "balloon mortgage"?**

A. A mortgage with fluctuating interest rates

B. A mortgage that requires a large final payment

C. A mortgage with no down payment

D. A mortgage paid off in less than 5 years

Answer: B

A balloon mortgage requires a large final payment at the end of the loan term.

➡ **45. What is "blockbusting"?**

A. Building multiple properties in a short time

B. Encouraging people to sell their homes by instigating fear of a changing neighborhood

C. The process of rezoning land

D. Buying large blocks of property for development

Answer: B

Blockbusting is the practice of encouraging people to sell their homes by instigating fear, often related to racial, ethnic, or social change in a neighborhood.

➡ **46. What is a "1031 exchange"?**

A. A tax-deferred property exchange

B. A type of mortgage loan

C. A property auction

D. An open house event

Answer: A

A 1031 exchange allows the owner to sell a property and reinvest the proceeds in a new property while deferring capital gains tax.

➡ **47. What is "eminent domain"?**

A. The right of the government to acquire private property for public use

B. The highest legal ownership of property

C. A type of zoning regulation

D. A clause in a mortgage contract

Answer: A

Eminent domain is the right of the government to acquire private property for public use, usually with compensation.

➠48. What is "equity" in real estate?

A. The market value of a property

B. The difference between the property's market value and the remaining mortgage balance

C. The initial down payment

D. The annual property tax

Answer: B

Equity is the difference between the market value of the property and the remaining balance on any loans secured by the property.

➠49. What is "escrow" in a real estate transaction?

A. A legal arrangement where a third party holds funds or documents

B. The initial offer made by a buyer

C. The final stage of mortgage approval

D. A type of home inspection

Answer: A

Escrow is a legal arrangement in which a third party temporarily holds funds or documents until the conditions of a contract are met.

➠50. What is "net operating income" in real estate investment?

A. Gross income minus operating expenses

B. Gross income plus operating expenses

C. Mortgage payments minus rental income

D. Property value minus mortgage balance

Answer: A

Net operating income is the gross income generated by a property minus the operating expenses, not including mortgage payments or taxes.

Day of the Exam

The day of the Washington Real Estate License Exam is a pivotal moment in your journey to becoming a licensed real estate professional. It's the culmination of months, or even years, of hard work, study, and preparation. This chapter aims to provide you with a comprehensive guide to navigate this crucial day successfully. From what to bring to the testing center to how to manage your time during the exam, we've got you covered.

Before the Exam Day

Final Review

In the week leading up to the exam, focus on reviewing key concepts, laws, and formulas that you've learned. Use flashcards, practice exams, and other study aids to reinforce your knowledge.

Test Center Location

Make sure you know the exact location of the test center. If possible, do a dry run to gauge how long it will take you to get there. This will help you plan your departure time on the exam day.

Sleep and Nutrition

A good night's sleep and proper nutrition can significantly impact your performance. Aim for at least 7-8 hours of sleep and eat a balanced meal before heading to the test center.

What to Bring

Identification

You will need to bring government-issued photo identification, such as a driver's license or passport. Make sure it's current and accurately reflects your name as it appears on your exam registration.

Exam Admission Ticket

Some testing centers require an admission ticket, which you may have received via email after registering for the exam. Print this out and bring it with you.

Supplies

Bring at least two pencils and a non-programmable calculator if the exam allows it. Check the specific rules for your testing center.

At the Test Center

Arrival Time

Arrive at least 30 minutes before your scheduled exam time. This will give you ample time to check-in and get settled.

Check-In Process

Upon arrival, you'll go through a check-in process that may include fingerprinting or other biometric verification. You'll also need to store your belongings in a designated area, as you're typically not allowed to bring anything into the exam room.

Pre-Exam Procedures

Before starting, you'll be given instructions on how to use the computer and navigate through the exam. Listen carefully and make sure you understand how to mark answers, skip questions, and review your work.

During the Exam

Time Management

The Washington Real Estate License Exam is divided into a national portion and a state-specific portion. Each has its own time limit. Keep an eye on the clock and pace yourself.

Question Strategy

Read each question carefully and eliminate incorrect answers when possible. If you're unsure about a question, mark it and return to it later.

Staying Calm

It's natural to feel nervous, but try to maintain your composure. Take deep breaths and focus on the questions, not the outcome.

After the Exam

Preliminary Results

In most cases, you'll receive preliminary results immediately after completing the exam. This will indicate whether you've passed or failed but is not the official result.

Official Results

Your official results will be sent to you via mail or will be available online within a few days to a week. This will include a breakdown of your performance in different subject areas.

Retaking the Exam

If you don't pass, don't despair. You'll receive information on how to retake the exam, including any waiting periods and additional fees.

Conclusion

The day of the Washington Real Estate License Exam is undoubtedly stressful, but with the right preparation and mindset, you can navigate it successfully. This chapter has provided you with a detailed roadmap for the day, from the moment you wake up to the moment you complete the exam. Remember, this is just one step in your real estate career journey, but it's a significant one. Good luck, and may your preparation and determination bring you the success you deserve.

After the Exam: Next Steps

Congratulations on completing the Washington Real Estate License Exam! Whether you've passed or need to retake the exam, this chapter will guide you through the critical steps to take after the exam. From understanding your results to planning your career, we'll cover all the essential aspects to set you on the right path.

Understanding Your Results

Preliminary Results

Immediately after the exam, you'll receive preliminary results. These are not your official scores but will give you an idea of your performance.

Official Results

Your official results will be mailed to you or made available online within a week. These results will include a detailed breakdown of your performance in various subject areas.

Score Breakdown

Understanding the score breakdown can help you identify your strengths and weaknesses. If you didn't pass, this information would be invaluable for your re-preparation.

If You Didn't Pass

Don't Panic

Failing the exam can be disheartening, but it's not the end of the world. Many successful real estate agents didn't pass on their first try.

Review Your Weak Areas

Use the score breakdown to identify the areas where you need improvement. Focus your study efforts on these topics.

Rescheduling the Exam

You'll need to wait for a specific period before you can retake the exam. Check the guidelines for retaking the exam in Washington, including any additional fees.

Re-Preparation

Consider enrolling in a prep course or hiring a tutor for areas where you struggled. Use practice exams to gauge your improvement.

If You Passed

Celebrate, But Stay Focused

Passing the exam is a significant achievement, but it's just the first step in your real estate career. Celebrate your success, but remember that there's more to do.

Apply for Your License

You'll need to submit an application to the Washington State Department of Licensing to receive your official real estate license. This will include submitting your exam scores, background check, and any required fees.

Join a Brokerage

Newly licensed agents must work under a licensed broker. Research different brokerages to find one that aligns with your career goals.

MLS and Association Membership

Consider joining your local Multiple Listing Service (MLS) and real estate associations. These memberships will provide you with valuable resources and networking opportunities.

Building Your Career

Networking

Start building your professional network immediately. Attend industry events, join real estate associations, and connect with experienced agents and brokers.

Marketing Yourself

Invest in business cards, a professional website, and social media presence. Consider specialized marketing courses to enhance your skills.

Continuing Education

Washington State requires real estate agents to complete continuing education courses for license renewal. Stay updated on this to ensure you meet the requirements.

Specialization

As you gain experience, consider specializing in a particular type of real estate, such as commercial properties, luxury homes, or property management.

Financial Planning

Commission Structure

Understand the commission structure at your brokerage. This will help you set realistic financial goals.

Expenses

As an agent, you'll have various expenses, including marketing costs, association fees, and possibly desk fees at your brokerage. Plan your budget accordingly.

Taxes

As a real estate agent, you're essentially a small business owner. Consult a tax advisor to understand your tax obligations and potential deductions.

Conclusion

The period following the Washington Real Estate License Exam is crucial for setting the stage for your career. Whether you passed or need to retake the exam, the steps you take now will significantly impact your future success. From understanding your exam results to making career and financial plans, this chapter has aimed to provide a comprehensive guide for navigating this critical period. Your journey in the real estate world is just beginning, and the opportunities are endless. Good luck, and may you find immense success in all your endeavors.

Career Development

Congratulations on passing the Washington Real Estate License Exam and taking the first steps into your new career! This chapter aims to be your comprehensive guide to career development in the real estate industry. From choosing a brokerage to mastering the art of negotiation, we'll cover the essential aspects of building a successful career.

Choosing the Right Brokerage

Types of Brokerages

Traditional Brokerages: These are the well-established firms that offer a full range of real estate services. They often provide training programs and marketing support but may charge higher fees.

Discount Brokerages: These firms offer limited services for a reduced commission. They are suitable for agents who prefer to handle most tasks themselves.

Virtual Brokerages: These are online platforms that offer agents flexibility. They often have lower overhead costs, which can mean fewer fees for agents.

What to Consider

Commission Split: Understand how the commission is divided between you and the brokerage.

Training and Support: Does the brokerage offer ongoing training, mentorship, and administrative support?

Reputation: A brokerage's reputation can significantly impact your career, especially when you're starting.

Building a Client Base

Networking

Personal Network: Start with friends and family and ask for referrals.

Online Presence: Utilize social media and real estate websites to generate leads.

Local Events: Attend community events to meet potential clients.

Customer Relationship Management (CRM)

Data Collection: Keep track of all interactions with potential and existing clients.

Follow-ups: Use the CRM to set reminders for follow-ups.

Email Marketing: Regular updates about the real estate market can keep you in clients' minds.

Marketing Strategies

Traditional Marketing

Flyers and Postcards: These can be effective for targeting a specific geographic area.

Newspaper Ads: Despite the digital age, many people still read newspapers.

Digital Marketing

Website: A professional website can serve as a portfolio of your services and listings.

Social Media: Platforms like Instagram and Facebook are excellent for showcasing properties.

SEO: Search engine optimization can help your website rank higher in search results.

Skill Development

Negotiation Skills

Active Listening: Understand your client's needs and concerns.

Be Prepared: Know the property details, market conditions, and possible objections.

Win-Win Situation: Aim for a deal that benefits both parties.

Time Management

Prioritize: Not all tasks are equally important.

Set Goals: Short-term and long-term goals can guide your daily activities.

Avoid Procrastination: Use tools and techniques to keep procrastination at bay.

Financial Planning

Budgeting

Income: Have a clear understanding of your income, including the commission splits and any other sources.

Expenses: These can include MLS fees, advertising costs, and transportation.

Savings: Always put aside a portion of your income for taxes and emergencies.

Taxes

Quarterly Taxes: As an independent contractor, you'll need to pay estimated taxes quarterly.

Deductions: Keep track of all business-related expenses for deductions.

Continuing Education and Licensing

State Requirements

Continuing Education: Washington State requires 30 hours of continuing education every two years for license renewal.

Legal Updates: Stay updated on any changes in real estate laws and regulations.

Additional Certifications

NAR's Green Designation: For agents interested in sustainable and green real estate.

Certified Residential Specialist (CRS): For agents who want to focus on residential real estate.

Conclusion

Career development in real estate is a continuous process that requires dedication, skill, and a bit of entrepreneurial spirit. From the moment you choose a brokerage to the time you close a deal, every step offers an opportunity for growth and improvement. This chapter has aimed to provide a comprehensive roadmap for your career journey in Washington's real estate market. Whether you're a new agent or looking to take your career to the next level, the strategies and tips outlined here can serve as your guide to success.

Conclusion

As you close the final pages of this book, you're not just ending a chapter in your educational journey; you're beginning a new chapter in your professional life. This book has aimed to be your comprehensive guide, covering everything from understanding the Washington real estate market to the intricacies of contracts, ethics, and even career development.

The real estate industry is ever-changing, influenced by economic trends, technological advancements, and legislative changes.

While this book provides a strong foundation, your learning should not stop here. Continuing education, both formal and informal, will be crucial as you navigate the complexities of the real estate world. Real estate is not just about properties; it's about people. The relationships you cultivate—with clients, fellow agents, and industry professionals—will be invaluable. Networking doesn't just help you in lead generation; it can also provide mentorship opportunities and professional growth. In this digital age, a plethora of tools are available to help you succeed. From CRM systems to digital marketing platforms, these tools can streamline your workflow and help you manage your time more effectively.

However, remember that while technology can aid you, the human element in real estate is irreplaceable. Your intuition, empathy, and ability to understand your client's needs are skills that no machine can replicate. As exciting as a career in real estate can be, it's essential to manage your finances wisely. Budgeting, saving, and understanding your taxes are crucial for long-term success. Equally important is maintaining the highest ethical standards. Passing the Washington Real Estate License Exam is a significant achievement, but it's just the first step. Your next steps could include finding a mentor, joining a reputable brokerage, or even starting your own agency. Thank you for allowing this book to be a part of your real estate journey. It has been designed not just to help you pass an exam but to prepare you for a fulfilling and successful career in real estate.

Here's to your future in Washington real estate—may it be as rewarding as it is promising!

Made in United States
Troutdale, OR
05/10/2024

19781664R00139